Michel Renouard

Wonderful Saint-Malo and the Emerald Coast

Photographs by Hervé Boulé
Translated by Angela Moyon

EDITIONS OUEST-FRANCE

13 rue du Breil, Rennes

By the same author (selection) :

Lumière sur Kerlivit, novel, 1964; repr. 1988, Saint-Vincent-sur-Oust, Ed. Elor.
Le Requin de Runavel (with J-F. Bazin), novel, 1990, Saint-Vincent-sur-Oust, Ed. Elor.
Le Chant des adieux, novel, 1976; repr. 1979.
Châtellerault, Ouest-France, 1986.
A New Guide to Brittany, Ouest-France, 1984.
Romanesque Art in Brittany, Ouest-France, 1980.
Brittany, Ouest-France, 1984.
Mon premier guide de Bretagne (drawings by C. Lazé), Ouest-France, 1987.
Wonderful Finistère, Ouest-France, 1988.
Wonderful Morbihan, Ouest-France, 1990.
Wonderful Ille-et-Vilaine, Ouest-France, 1990.
Marco Polo, Ed. Gisserot, 1990.
La Bible, Ed. Gisserot, 1988.

Opposite : *Dinan : The clock tower.*

Front cover : *Saint-Malo.*

Back cover : *Dinan Harbour seen c. 1835 by a painter from Marseilles, Isidore Dagnan (1794-1873). The Emerald Valley is suffused in a golden light here which is rather more Mediterranean than Breton. (Dinan Museum collection).*

The harbour in Saint-Malo.

INTRODUCTION

Eastern Brittany, the Emerald Coast. Emerald Land, and, why not, Emerald Triangle, taking the three outermost points of Erquy, Dinan and Cancale. Words flow from the pen like grains of sand between the fingers. Names have no distinct limits. They form a contrast. They are complementary.

There are those who talk about the north-west of Ille-et-Vilaine and the east of Côtes d'Armor. Others use even less poetic markers such as districts or sub-districts. Certain authors make use of convenient but intangible entities such as "the

Saint-Malo area", the "Dinan area", the "Fréhel area". Historians will tell you that this is first and foremost the land of the Coriosolites. Charters in hand, priests will talk of the bishoprics of Saint-Malo, Dol and Saint-Brieuc. A few eccentrics even prefer terms such as Poudouvre or Clos-Poulet. Emerald green obviously has more than one hue.

Any choice is arbitrary. Some readers may find this guide book too restrictive; others will find the choice too wide-ranging. The author has merely attempted to include in this book all the areas

in Eastern Brittany that look seawards, the areas whose destiny was played out along the Channel coasts. Even in Dinan, Pluduno or Plancoët, the Emerald Coast never seems to be more than a few miles away.

The coastal strip that we have selected, jagged as the teeth of a saw, stretches from Erquy to Saint-Benoît-des-Ondes to the south of Cancale. It is true that the name Emerald Coast *is usually even more restricting since it covers the area from Cap Fréhel to Cancale. But it is impossible to discuss Fréhel without mentioning Sables-d'Or-*

3

les-Pins and Erquy, just as it is impossible to talk about Cancale without including its hinterland.

Inland, it was easy to draw the border. The Poudouvre is bounded by two rivers, the Rance and Arguenon, each of them pulsating to the rhythm of the tides. The Rance Valley in particular was, for many years, the main source of communication between the Channel and the inland rural areas. When storms lashed the sea, the peasants around Dinan held their breath, for every second local lad was a ship's boy or sailor.

In the days of Antiquity, the Rance Valley also linked the bustling capital of the Coriosolites, Corseul, to Normandy and the remainder of Gaul, through the river port at Taden and its ford. Corseul's merchants were by no means stay-at-homes and their coinage has been found on Jersey and in England. Facing the Rance and the sea, Corseul also justifies its place in our study of the Emerald Land, even if the Coriosolite territory actually stretched much further south and west.

And westward, since we are talking of it, there is Fréhel, the hyphen between Poudouvre and Penthièvre (the Lamballe area). The tiny Frémur flows bravely into the Baie de la Fresnaye, where the harbours were once used by Knights Templar who had settled in the locality, in a part of Brittany that was strongly affected by French, Norman and English influence.

Is this Emerald Triangle really Breton ? There's no doubt that it is and the place names are there to remind us of the fact. Some 1,000 years ago, the area was bilingual yet nowadays it comes as a surprise to find a large number of localities, rivers and hamlets with names of Breton origin, from Aucaleuc to Pleur-

Cancale as the hours pass.

Opposite : *Midsummer day's dream in Saint-Malo.*

tuit, and including Créhen, Coëtquen, Mordreuc, Plancoët, Frémur and Arguenon. In fact, it is in the very nature of this area of communication to be bilingual, Breton-French first and French-Gallo thereafter, and even, from the early 19th century *onwards, French-English in towns such as Saint-Malo, Dinard and Dinan where a large British colony edited* The Dinan Magazine *c. 1860.*

Brittany is often defined in terms of the exceptional density of its artistic and architectural

The bay off Saint-Malo.

heritage, but this seems to be less true in the Emerald Land. Nevertheless, the region has two towns whose architecture is, for various reasons, quite outstanding viz. Saint-Malo which suffered extensive damage in 1944 and, most of all, Dinan. It also has fine churches, castles, manorhouses, and more than one hundred malouinières, *rural mansions, some of which are absolute gems. This, though, is relatively little compared to other regions in Brittany such as Léon or Cornouaille.*

Even as regards literary output, the slight reserve of the local people comes as somewhat of a surprise. It is true that a literary genius, Chateaubriand, was born in Saint-Malo. And Lamennais was one of the greatest thinkers of his century. There were also some foremost novelists such as Roger Vercel. A few highly-reputed people such as Duclos, a member of the French Academy, Hippolyte de La Morvonnais or Théophile Briant are sometimes mentioned, but does anyone still read their works today? More recently, writers filled with inspiration like Jean Cordelier seemed to have a brilliant career in front of them but the Parisian publishing world condemned them to silence.

There are, nevertheless, a few poets who deserve a mention, e.g. Marie-Paule Salonne, Angèle Vannier, Bernard Colonne or Yves Prié. It is also interesting to note that most novels set in this area have been written by authors from elsewhere such as Raoul de Navery from Morbihan, the Anglo-Canadian Robert Service, Roger Vercel a native of Le Mans, Paul Vimereu from Picardy or the American of Scottish extraction Helen MacInnes. Not to mention Colette or Danielle Delouche, a native of Brest. But this is normal, for the eye of the novelist (or the painter) needs to stand back from the subject matter.

Herring gulls.

Great local artists are few and far between, despite the fact that the area has unceasingly attracted artists from other regions and lands. Yves Floc'h was born in Finistère, Yvonne Jean-Haffen, a follower of Mathurin Méheut, was more than forty years old when she settled on the shores of the R. Rance, André Mack was born in Saint-Brieuc, Claude Marin came from Nantes, and Daniel Derveaux from Paris. The pianist Henri Kowalski was Polish on his father's side and Breton on his mother's. Among the truly local artists, there are Pierre Rochereau, Guy Mahé, Alain Aurégan, Monik Rabasté, Louis Guillard and Jean-Luc Chauvin. Musical claims to fame are impressive but few in number - Théodore Botrel, a popular songster, Louis Aubert and Ivan Devriès, who wrote symphonic works, Myrdhin for the harp and Maripol who wrote poetic songs.

This area of transit, the junction between Brittany and Normandy, delighted those who came in search of beauty. From every direction, pedigree birds landed here, made their nests, and were content to stay. Writers or artists such as Luigi Odorici, Yvonne Jean-Haffen, Jacques Petit or André Mussat became Breton to the very depths of their souls. They did even more for their adopted region than many locals have done. It was Roger Vercel, for instance, who brought back to life, through the magic of fiction, the prodigious epic of the Cape Horners.

The truth is that this Emerald Coast is first and foremost a place of action and adventure. Mention travelling, trade, war-mongering, sailing the seas, conquering distant lands, or converting pagan countries, and the Bretons from this corner of Armorica were first in the queue. During the Crusades, they set off for the Holy Land. Then, over the

Léhon.

Saint-Servan : the old town of Aleth.

centuries, they were to be found in Asia, Africa, Canada, Newfoundland, Cape Horn or the Spanish Americas. They were seafarers, soldiers, explorers, missionaries, colonial leaders, navy surgeons or cartographers. The people of Saint-Malo, of course, had the lion's share of maritime history. One of their sons discovered Canada. Others settled offshore from Argentina, on the islands that became known in French as the "Malouines" (the Falklands). Privateers from Saint-Malo were seen on every ocean. From Dinan, Auguste Pavie set off to explore distant Indochina. Dr. François Broussais travelled throughout Europe with Napoleon's armies,

Dinan : Rue Jerzual.

In Saint-Malo.

and was at the Emperor's side at Austerlitz.

Those who stayed behind did not waste their time writing sonnets or madrigals. They put up their shop signs and counted their takings. Some of them became so rich, said Chateaubriand, that "when they had had one too many, they fried up piastres, and threw them out the window, boiling hot, down to the poor below in the street". *The "Gentlemen of Saint-Malo", whose prodigiously epic tale has been told by the historian André Lespagnol, were both adventurers and wily merchants.*

Even those who preferred spiritual adventure remained

men (and women) of action. The name of Jean-Marie de Lamennais is now known in some twenty countries. Jeanne Jugan, founder of the Order of the Little Sisters of the Poor, is venerated in over thirty countries. The Sisters of Divine Providence, whose congregation was founded by Guy Homéry, are present in countries as different as Zaire and Peru. A monk from Saint-Briac, Henri Le Saux, set off for India one day and founded an ashram there. And a brief look at the diocesan records in Rennes and Saint-Brieuc soon shows that many of the area's churchmen and women are still to be found today at the other ends of the earth. All of them responded, in their own way, to the call of adventure.

In fact, you only have to travel the world to know that there are always, be it in Nairobi, Benares, or Paramaribo, two or three Bretons around who were born in the Erquy-Dinan-Cancale triangle. On our maritime headland, contemplatives and poets are less commonplace than old salts, missionaries and globetrotters. Is it really by chance that the word emerald, which came from the Far East via Greece, was chosen to describe this area in which the rising sun is an invitation to take to the sea?

Most guidebooks on Brittany tend not to dwell on the Emerald Coast. They mention its main beauty spots in passing and describe its main monuments. On the spot, of course, local sages have carried out useful work, compiling and sifting through information. A few authors such as M-E. Monier (1901-1974) went one better and they were remarkable pioneers. University teachers have studied various aspects of the region, in line with their specialist subject. Yet major works of synthesis based on authentic historical research are few and far between. André Lespagnol's book on Saint-Malo is all the more precious for this, but Dinan is still awaiting its professional historian.

There is much still to be discovered about Eastern Brittany, this Emerald crescent drawn by the gods where, in the spindrift from the sea, ocean and rock continue to face each other, like the setting of our humblest moments and the sands of our most unlikely dreams.

The Château des Chênes near Saint-Malo.

ARCHITECTURE

The oldest remaining building is the Gallo-Roman **cella** (Temple of Mars) in Corseul, which was probably built at the end of the 1st century. Here and there, you may find traces of human settlements, but they are often half-concealed structures that are of interest only to specialists and archaeologists, or to those involved in aerial surveys. They are, though, more spectacular in Saint-Servan.

The architecture in the Emerald Coast area is first and foremost, **civil and military architecture**. There are a number of remarkable examples in Saint-Malo and even more in Dinan (houses with porches, private mansions, mediaeval streets, the Rue du Jerzual). The region has several fortresses (Saint-Servan, Fort-la-Latte, Bien-Assis) but a few of them lie in ruins (Montafilan, Montbran, Le Guildo, Coëtquen). The town walls in Dinan, the only ones of their kind in Brittany, run over a distance of almost two miles. Taden contains a rare 14th-century manorhouse. The shores of the R. Rance are bristling with manors and *malouinières*, most of them on the right bank.

Religious architecture is mainly Romanesque in style (West Front of St. Saviour's Basilica in Dinan, nave of the cathedral in Saint-Malo, Romanesque doorways in Créhen, Saint-Germain in Matignon and Saint-Lormel, or the church in St. Lunaire). Léhon has an old abbey, Saint-Suliac a very rare 13th-century church. Gothic architecture is visible in St. Malo's Church in Dinan and in the town of Saint-Malo. The remains of the oldest stained glass window in Brittany can be seen in Léhon (mid 13th century) and the Evangelists' Window in St. Saviour's in Dinan is an admirable work dating from the late 15th century. There are some fine modern windows in Notre-Dame du Temple (Pléboulle) and in the cathedral in Saint-Malo.

On the roadsides, there are numerous wayside crosses, but the only two monuments worthy

Pléhérel : the Vieux-Bourg chapel.

of note are in the village of Saint-Esprit (Léhon) and La Roche-au-Cygron (Fréhel).

R. ARGUENON

Arguenon comes from the Breton meaning "white river". It serves as a frontier between the Penthièvre (Lamballe area) and the Poudouvre (Dinan area). The R. Arguenon rises in the Gouray, i.e. near the sources of the Rance, and flows over 31 miles, crossing a number of towns and villages including Jugon before reaching Plancoët.

At this point along its course, it is canalised and is then navigable (the tide rises as far as Plancoët). It then flows on to Saint-Lormel, Créhen and Saint-Cast (the harbour of Le Guildo) before coming to rest at the foot of Gilles of Brittany's castle. It was here that François Ménez rediscovered, "the inexpressible softness steeped in sadness of the Trégor's "river beds" which, beneath the ashen polish of their mists, impose their peace-giving silence on souls".

The entire area between Plancoët and Le Guildo is filled with pacles for outings, in the midst of a natural environment which has, miraculously, escaped unscathed.

BAIE DE LA FRESNAYE
(Côtes d'Armor)

The Baie de la Fresnaye is one of the most prestigious beauty spots on the Emerald Coast. It is interesting both as a place to visit and as a place to be studied in detail. Bounded to the west by the Fréhel headland and to the east by the Saint-Cast peninsula, it is fed from the south by the waters of the Frémur. It is almost 4 miles deep and is roughly rectangular in shape.

Regulated by the ebb and flow of the tides, the bay has four tiny harbours viz. Port-Saint-Céran (to the NW), Port-Nieux (to the W), Port-à-la-Duc (to the S) and Port-Saint-Jean (to the E). A heather-lined footpath (once a customs path) crosses the entire area, from Les Sables-d'Or to Port-à-la-Duc.

La Fresnaye.

From there, you can walk on to the headland at La Corbière (Saint-Cast), via Crissouët and Sainte-Efficace.

Mussel and oyster farming have become two of the bay's main activities. Shellfish gather-

The Verger Beach in Cancale.

ing is authorised at low tide. While you are busy, try recognising a few of the birds. They are all the more numerous here because the cliffs and islets along Cap Fréhel are one of the main nature reserves on the north coast.

CANCALE (Ille-et-Vilaine)
9 miles E of Saint-Malo

Brittany has two harbours with apparently similar etymology - Concarneau and Cancale. In both cases, the first syllable, *konk* (cf. Latin *concha*) is said to mean a creek or bay. The name Cancale is said to have been derived from Konkaven and, later, Konkall but the meaning of the end of the word remains uncertain.

Cancale.

The bay was created by a series of invasions by the sea. Tradition has it that a tidal wave covered the Scissy Forest in 709 A.D. and that the rocks of Cancale are the remains of the sunken shoreline.

The fishing harbour gained fame from its oysters. Before the French Revolution, they were taken to Versailles twice a week and served at the King's table. The seafood aroused envy and English fishermen had no hesitation in coming to pillage the oysterbeds. It was, though, more paticularly the British Navy which the local people feared. In 1758, the Duke of Marlborough's fleet attacked and pillaged the port. Twenty years later, the English bombarded it again. Today, the

Pointe du Grouin.

beds in the Baie du Mont Saint-Michel have been decimated, and the oyster farmers buy their brood stock from Belon.

Cancale was the birthplace of the founder of the Little Sisters of the Poor, a fisherman's daughter, the Blessed Jeanne Jugan (1792-1879). Another of Cancale's famous sons and daughters was Eugène Royer (b. 1921) who has written a number of books about Brittany.

To the north is a cliffside path leading to the Pointe du Grouin. It's a wonderful path and, in clear weather, you can see the outline of Mont Saint-Michel. Beyond the Pointe de la Chaîne opposite the **Ile des Rimains** (the fort dates from 1782), you reach the cove at Port-Briac, the shore at Port-Pican, the beach at Port-Mer, then the **Pointe du Grouin**. The spray-soaked headland is a remarkable sight during the storms that accompany the September equinox. The **Ile des Landes** is a bird sanctuary (black cormorants). From the Pointe du Grouin, the path leads on to the Du-Guesclin Cove (cf. Saint-Coulomb).

Profoundly marked by fishing which, not so long ago, still took men away from home for periods of between 7 and 11 months every year, the Cancale area is a world apart, of interest to psychologist and sociologist alike. Within the home, it is often the women (rather than the sea captains) who stick their oars in and rule the family. The **museum** in the former St. Meen's Church is a good introduction to the microcosm of Cancale and its history. And be sure not to miss the amazing festivities held on the waterfront (**La Houle**) on August 15th. Dozens of resting-places are set up there and, when evening comes, groups of local people come to sing old psalms while, on the same day, wherever they may be on seas and oceans throughout the world, fishermen from Cancale can be heard singing the same psalms.

The parish church is fairly recent (1886) and its tower can serve as a lookout post. From it, the view stretches over the coast and the Baie du Mont Saint-Michel. Notre-Dame du Verger

Cancale.

Chapel, which was rebuilt in 1833, was once the setting for a famous *pardon,* or religious procession.

In days gone by, the Granville, Cancale and Rance areas were famous for their "bisquines" (fishing smacks that came originally from the Bay of Biscay). A new bisquine, the *Cancalaise,* was launched on 18th April 1987.

LES CHAMPS-GERAUX
(Côtes d'Armor)
6 miles SE of Dinan

This is still a very "young" community, created in 1934. It lies within the Dinan area. Part of the Coëtquen Forest (cf. Saint-Hélen) is situated within the village boundary. The R. Rance flows past Le Vaugré.

A visit to Les Champs-Géraux could not be motivated by artistic reasons, even though there are several fine manor-farmhouses here dating from the 17th and 18th centuries, a chateau (La Gravelle) and Notre-Dame Chapel (18th century). The unusual feature of this community lies elsewhere. The village of **Fautrel** on the very edge of the forest is one of the last places in which *craquelins* are produced in a traditional small-scale manner !

This activity has existed in the area for hundreds of years but over the last few decades it has become increasingly rare. As their name suggests, *craquelins* are dry pastry puffs made with flour and eggs which crackle as you eat them. In the Middle Ages, they were also known as "*échaudés*" (scalded buns) because the dough was scalded with simmering water. The shape has chan-

Cracknel making in Les Champs-Géraux.

ged depending on the period and the area. In Dinan, they are round with raised edges.

The proximity of the Coëtquen Forest is not mere chance. In days gone by, *craquelin*-makers used wood-fired ovens.

The inhabitants of Les Champs-Géraux are known as Champs-Gérausiens or Campos-Gérausiens.

CHATEAUNEUF-D'ILLE-ET-VILAINE (Ille-et-Vilaine)
9 miles S of Saint-Malo

Of the castle, which has suffered many misfortunes since the 11th century, all that remains is one ruined **tower** (15th century) out of the original six. Nearby is another, 17th-century castle. Renée de Rieux was born here in 1550. She charmed the court and the future King Henri II. Ever since her death, she has haunted the park in Châteauneuf. If you listen very carefully at night, you can hear her dress rustling over the paving-stones.

The Château de la Basse-Motte to the west of the town dates from the 18th century. To the east, the **Saint-Coulban Pond** (also known as Saint-Coulman) was once an arm of the sea. When the Channel swamped the Scissy Forest, the Clos-Poulet area became an island. The R. Rance then flowed into the bay at Cancale. The entire area of swampland filled a vast triangle bounded by Châteauneuf, Saint-Guinoux and Lillemer. It is one of the natural boundaries of the Clos-Poulet but its size varies depending on the season.

Every evening, you can hear a deep roar, the Saint-Coulban bellow. Some say it is a heron; others believe it to be the groans of souls in purgatory. There are even those who speak of a beast of the depths, a Breton cousin of the Loch Ness monster. But having checked out these stories, it turned out to be the moan of the dragon tamed by St. Suliac (cf. Saint-Suliac).

The *Chanson d'Aquin*, a 12th-century romance, tells how the town of Gardoine was swallowed up by the waves at this spot. When occupied by the Saracen, Charlemagne asked God to destroy the fortress. His prayers were answered and the town was submerged.

Pierre Rochebonne (1885-1946), who was born in Châteauneuf, was a sailor before becoming a railwayman - and writer. His best-known work is *La Sirène de la Rance : roman de la Côte d'Emeraude* (1925) in which most of the action takes place on the shores of the R. Rance.

Châteauneuf.

LE CLOS-POULET
(Ille-et-Vilaine)

The Clos-Poulet (i.e. the enclosure of the Alet area) lies between the Rance to the west, the Channel to the north and the Baie du Mont Saint-Michel to the east. Its southern boundary is less well-defined but corresponds more or less to a diagonal running between Saint-Benoît-des-Ondes along the Biez Jean towards the pond at Saint-Coulban and on to the shores of the R. Rance south of La Ville-es-Nonais. Some authors extend it even further, to Pleudihen.

The district, then, is a large coastal area covering Saint-Malo and Cancale, the entire right bank of the R. Rance from Saint-Servan to La Ville-es-Nonais, and a rich hinterland around Saint-Méloir where the main activity is market gardening.

In addition to the wide range of natural beauty spots along the Rance and the coast, the Clos-Poulet has an unusually high number of castles, manorhouses and *malouinières* (more than one hundred in all), as well as artistic or architectural treasures in towns such as Saint-Malo and Saint-Suliac.

Chateaubriand described the atmosphere in the Clos-Poulet when its splendour was at its height, "A continual blend of rocks and greenery, shoreline and forests, creeks and hamlets, ancient manors of feudal Brittany and modern dwellings of the Brittany of merchants."

The Temple of Mars in Corseul.

CORSEUL (Côtes d'Armor)
6 miles W of Dinan

The territory of the Coriosolites, with its main town, Corseul, entered the history books in 57 B.C. when Julius Caesar mentioned it in his *Gallic Wars*. All that is known about this Gallic tribe is that it minted its own coinage, owned Jersey, and traded with southern Britain. From c. 40 B.C. onwards, Corseul became a Roman township, probably (but there is some doubt about this) called Fanum Martis before taking the name of Civitas Coriosolitum in the 3rd century A.D.

For four hundred years, Corseul was a Gallo-Roman settlement of no little importance. Five Roman roads led to the town and Corseul traded with an area of the Roman Empire stretching from Aquitaine to Tuscany. It was especially prosperous during the latter part of the 1st century A.D. under the leadership of Vespasian, Titus and Domitian. It had a forum, baths, monuments, and temples. The Coriosolites had adopted the Greco-Roman gods (Cybele, Mars) without foregoing the worship of Celtic deities (Sirona). Decline set in in the early years of the 4th century. And soon, Alet (cf. Saint-Malo) supplanted the former capital of the Coriosolites. The barbarians dealt the town a death blow and it was apparently burnt down in 406 A.D.

There are few reminders of this era. Over the centuries, the Roman remains were pillaged (in the 18th century, stones from Corseul were used to build the ramparts in Saint-Malo). A few fragments, including a 6 1/2 ft. high column topped by a capital, have been brought together in the gardens around the town hall. There are others (bases of columns) in the Garden of Antiquities in the Rue Lessard. Nearby is an **archaeological museum**.

The church (1838) contains a rare **stoop** supported by caryatids said to date from the 12th century. Its most outstanding feature, however, is a **Gallo-Roman tombstone** bearing an inscription in capital letters. It is built into the corner of the south wall to the right of the chancel (details of the lettering are shown up by a light working on a time switch). According to the writer Prosper Mérimée, the text reads, "*Dedicated to the deified spirits of the dead. Here lies Sicilia Namgidde who, motivated by admirable tenderness, followed her son from her country, Africa. She lived 65 years. Cneius Flavius Januarius, her son, erected this tomb in her memory*".

Some 200 yds. from the church on the Saint-Jacut road is the **Champ-Mulon** dig. But the only spectacular monument is approximately 2 miles east of the town hall on the Dinan road, in the village of Haut-Bécherel. It is a *cella*, known as the **Temple of Mars**. The polygonal tower, which was probably built in the latter part of the 1st century A.D. is evidence of the high quality and solidity of Roman buildings.

In the opposite direction, i.e. some 2 miles west of the town hall, a narrow lane leads from the centre of Corseul to **Montafilan Castle** (late 12th - early 13th century, with 14th-century alterations), which was probably built on the site of a Roman fort. It is here that an altar dedicated to the goddess Sirona was found (it is now in the museum in Dinan). The castle was built of stone from Corseul and when the keep fell down, the stones were used to build the new church.

Stones live on; civilisations die.

The ruins of Montafilan Castle in Corseul.

CREHEN (Côtes d'Armor)
12 miles NW of Dinan

The village on the banks of the R. Arguenon is built on a hill, which may explain how it got its name (from the Breton *krec'h* or *krec'hienn*, meaning "a hill"). This is a fairly common placename (it can be found again in Pleurtuit, for example). The **church** is modern (1817-1832) but some parts of its (the door) came from a Romanesque building.

In the village is the parent convent of the Sisters of Divine Providence of Créhen (which has also beer a girls' school since 1913). The congregation was founded by Father Guy Homéry (1781-1861) who became parish priest in Créhen in 1818. It now has some 560 sisters throughout the world (France, Belgium, Netherlands, Peru and Zaire).

Bréjerac Manor on the Ploubalay road dates from the 15th century but was altered in later times. More difficult to find is the **Château de la Touche-à-la-Vache** (15th century but with much older features said to date from the 13th century). All that remains of it today is a pile of ruins - and an unusual name.

Other remains, like those of Le Guildo Casle to the north-west, also lie within the Créhen parish boundary but it seemed more logical to include them under Saint-Cast-le-Guildo.

Duchess Anne Keep in Dinan.

DINAN (Côtes d'Armor)
32 miles NW of Rennes

Dinan is, along with Carcassonne, one of France's most attractive walled towns. Its geographical setting is quite exceptional. Instead of nestling on the valley floor like Morlaix, most of Dinan's urban development has been on the hillside. Thus the town overlooks the 225 ft. drop down to the R. Rance. The most fascinating view of the town with its viaduct, ramparts, towers and belfries is to be had from the Rennes road. And when you actually reach the old town, you will find churches, chapels, former monasteries, houses with carriage entrances and pillars, and narrow streets with ill-fitting cobblestones. Nor does this mark the end of the list of riches and places of interest in the former capital of the Poudouvre (q.v.). The Coriosolites (cf. Corseul) occupied the hill. Then came the Romans who were probably the first inhabitants to build real fortifications (the Corseul-Avranches road passed close to Dinan). And c. 1065, William the Conqueror laid siege to the wooden castle that had replaced the Roman fort.

Several writers and artists were born in Dinan or spent some part of their lives there e.g. Auguste

Pavis (1847-1925) who spent 28 years exploring south-east Asia before writing several books on the subject; the chronicler Louis-Gabriel Pringué (1883-1963); the psychologist André Le Gall (b. 1904; the novelists Jean Cordelier (1913-1980), Simone Vercel (b. 1923) and Yves Jacob (b. 1940), or again Tanguy Kenec'hdu (b. 1914) who translated the works of Yukio Mishima; the painter Alain Aurégan (b. 1941); the writer Hervé Carn (b. 1949); the musician Myrdhin (b. 1950); and the journalist Jean-Yves Ruaux (b. 1951), a Korean expert. The poet and chronicler Jacques Petit (b. 1922) has been living in Dinan since 1944. And in the last century, when he was a student in Rennes, Charles Leconte de l'Isle often came to Dinan, which was his father's birthplace, and there he feel deeply in love with a young English girl.

Indeed, for some 150 years, the town had a colony of British subjects, many of them retired Army officers (140 residents in 1842, 502 in 1870). Dinan even had its own quarterly English language magazine. Lord Kitchener's family lived in the country nearby and Lawrence of Arabia paid several visits to the area between 1893 and 1908 (cf. Dinard). In 1942, an American writer of Scots descent, Helen MacInnes, wrote a novel entitled *Assignment in Brittany*, the first work of fiction dealing with the Resistance Movement in Brittany.

In the summer, driving in Dinan is difficult; parking is even more problematical. Meters and ticket machines in car parks prevent long stops. The easiest way to overcome this problem is to get to Dinan at the crack of dawn and leave the car (if you are coming from Rennes, turn left at the end of the viaduct) on the car

park around the equestrian statue of Du Guesclin by the Parisian sculptor Emmanuel Frémiet (b. 1902). Although Du Guesclin was actually born in Broons, he was a Dinannais at heart. He met his first wife, Tiphaine Raguenel, here.

And it was here, in 1359, that he fought an Englishman who had kept his brother prisoner during a truce. The duel took place on the nearby **Place du Champ**.

From the square, go up the Rue Sainte-Claire to the Place du

Rue de l'Apport, Dinan.

The Rance Valley.

Théâtre. The pillared house on the left of the square is the 16th-century **Kératry House**, now the Tourist Office. The building actually comes from Lanvollon near Saint-Brieuc where it lay in ruins after a fire. It was brought to Dinan in 1938. A few yards away, the **Théâtre des Jacobins** stands on the site of the convent founded in 1224; a few remains of the original building can be seen inside. Near the theatre, in the Rue Pavie, is a Renaissance gateway that has been rebuilt after being brought here from a private chapel in Saint-André-des-Eaux.

Not far away is the Rue de l'Horloge with its 15th and 16th century houses and, more especially, its late 15th-century **belfry**. It is some 195 ft. high and contains four bells, the largest of which was a gift from Duchess Anne of Brittany. Beneath the tower is a small shopping centre

The cloisters in the Franciscan friary.

built in 1985 which has been a commercial success.

Turn back and take the Rue de Léhon which has two 18th-century houses (the Montmuran and France residences). Beyond them is the chapel (1662) of the former Benedictine convent (18th century). In 1934, at the request of the then headmaster, Antoine Gouze (who was to become François Mitterand's father-in-law), the chapel was turned into the gymnasium for the **Roger Vercel Secondary School**, named after one of its teachers, Roger Vercel (1894-1957) who was awarded the Goncourt Literary Prize in 1934. From 1777 to 1791, the convent had already been used as a private school, the Collège des Laurents. Two of Saint-Malo's famous sons, Dr. Robert Broussais (who has given his name to a hospital in Paris, cf. Pleurtuit) and the writer Chateaubriand were pupils there. The school dining hall contains 17th-century frescoes.

Further on is the St. Louis Gate (1620), the most recent of the town's gateways. From the other side, there is a general view of the "castle". Dinan had been without a fortress for one hundred years when, in the late 14th century, Duke John IV gave orders for the building of **Duchess Anne's Tower**. It is 110 ft. high. The title of "castle" (which is, in fact, something of a misnomer) was given to the building by Philippe de Mercoeur, Governor of Brittany and leader of the Leaguers. He had this tower and the Coëtquen Tower (15th century) beyond it linked by a redoubt that would withstand attack from without - and within (it pays to be careful). Today, it houses a very interesting **Museum**. The Porte du Guichet (14th century), a gateway flanked by towers, forms the entrance to the castle. But only during the **Ramparts Festival** can visitors walk the length of the town's walls.

At the foot of the keep is the **Promenade des Petits-Fossés**, built on the former counterscarp. Below it is a 10-acre park surrounding the public library (50,000 books), an ornithological museum, and a children's play area, the Jardin des Petits-Diables (Little Devils' Garden). At the top of a gloomy column erected

The tourist office and the Clock Tower.

The Jerzual Gate.

Opposite, top : *The Old Bridge.*

Opposite, bottom : *Rue de l'Apport and Rue de l'Horloge.*

in 1838, Charles Duclos (1704-1772) continues his silent monologue in utter disillusionment. He was a novelist and a contributor to Diderot's "Encyclopaedia" - but nobody reads his works today.

Opposite this bust, the narrow alleyway known as the Trou-au-Chat leads to the town centre. Take the **Rue de la Cordonnerie** on the left; it is bordered by 15th-century houses with oriel windows. The street runs down to the Place des Merciers, on which stands **Old Mother Pourcel's House** (now a restaurant) containing a remarkable 16th-century

wooden staircase. A few yards away, at 10 Rue de la Mittrie, is the birthplace of song-writer Théodore Botrel (1868-1925).

Turn back to the Place des Cordeliers which, despite the terrible fire of February 1907, still has a few arcaded houses (16th century) and the 15th-century gateway to the **Cordeliers' Monastery** which was closed down in 1791. It had been founded c. 1245 by the Lord of Dinan, Henri d'Avaugour, on his return from the Crusades. There is nothing left of the original Franciscan sanctuary and most of the build-

ings were completed in the 15th century. The most noteworthy examples of this period are the cloisters and courtyard. The **Chapter House** (also 15th century) is now used as one of the dining halls for the school which replaced the Franciscan monastery in January 1803 after having been evicted from its premises in the Rue de Léhon during the French Revolution. The Chapter House was twice used as a meeting place for Brittany's States General, the itinerant regional parliament. Opposite the chapel (1903) is the 16th-century apse of

St. Malo's Church, a flamboyant bouquet of stonework. To get to it, turn right just outside the gateway of the school.

Nearby, at 4 Grand'Rue is the remarkable 59-foot high six-sided turret on the **Plouër Residence** (early 16th century but with some 18th-century additions). It was there that conspirators planned the liberation of Dinan from the Leaguers in February 1598, thereby preparing the way for King Henri IV's visit to Brittany in March and the signing of the Edict of Nantes in April. In 1773, the house became the winter residence of the Count of Plouër, whose wife was Chateaubriand's godmother. The building then underwent a series of misfortunes. It has been part of the school since 1927.

Beyond the house is **St. Malo's Church** on which work began in 1489. It is built in the Flamboyant Gothic style but was not completed until 1865. On the south side is a double Renaissance doorway. Inside, note the chancel with its ambulatory and radiating chapels, based on the style of architecture common in Normandy. At the end of the nave (1855), is a 19th-century stoop supported by Satan. Merklan's stained glass windows (c. 1925) are certainly not lacking in colour.

Take the Rue de la Boulangerie and the Rue des Quatre-Miches on the north side of the church (Kitchener's family lived at no. 9 Rue des Quatre-Miches) and you will arrive at the Promenade des Grands-Fossés which runs partway along the ramparts. Turn right up the counterscarp (Cours Verdun) and you will reach the

Top : *St. Malo's Church.*
Bottom : *Rue Jerzual.*

Criticism Bench (it is often very busy), the Alloué (or Beaumanoir) Tower, and finally the 14th-century **St. Malo Gate**. Beyond it are the Rue de l'Ecole and the Rue de la Poissonnerie. At the corner of this street and the Rue de la Lainerie is the **Trinitarians' House** said to date from c. 1368 but with major alterations. Opposite, in the Rue de la Lainerie, is the remarkable **Patru Mansion** (1774) probably the last colonnaded house to be built in Dinan. Not far away is the Rue du Jerzual but first of all go on towards the clock tower and the **Place de l'Apport** with its exceptional group of arcaded houses (all of them renovated).

On the left as you go down the Rue Haute-Voie is a Renaissance gateway topped by four dolphins. It opens onto the **Beaumanoir Mansion** (1535) which was a Dominican convent in the 17th century. It was damaged by fire during the last war but has now been restored.

The narrow Rue de la Larderie leads to **St. Saviour's Basilica**. Every century from the Romanesque period onwards has left its mark on this church. The lower part of the West Front (note the projecting sculptures of winged creatures above the modern tympanum) and the south side wall date from the 12th century. The campanile on the tower was erected in 1779. The church was largely rebuilt in the late 15th and 16th centuries but has never really been finished (there is one side aisle missing). The interior is dark and oppressive but not devoid of interest. Note the font

Top : *The Beaumanoir Residence.*

Bottom : *The Romanesque West Front of St. Saviour's Basilica.*

Opposite : *St. Saviour's Basilica : the Evangelists' Window.*

(12th century), the Evangelists' Window (15th century), the Rosary Reredos, and the nearby Empire-period cenotaph which has contained Bertrand Du Guesclin's heart since 1810, the huge canopied High Altar (18th century), and the 16th-century

Dinan-Lanvallay : the viaduct.

chancel. Behind the chancel, there are two Romanesque capitals on pedestals, and to the right is a picture of Our Lady of All Virtues (16th century).

The **English Gardens** lie beyond the church near the old town walls high above the R. Rance. To the right of the gardens is the 17th-century Catherinettes' Convent which became a hospice in 1816. A **viaduct** (812 ft. long and 130 ft. high) has straddled the river valley since 1852. From the English Gardens, take the Rue du Rampart and the Rue Michel; this will bring you to the **Rue du Jerzual** and its continuation, the **Rue du Petit Port**, which runs down to the harbour. The two streets are separated by the Jerzual Gate (14th-15th centuries); both wind their way down between rows of houses. Much of

A glass-spinner in Dinan.

Rue du Petit-Port.

the property here has been bought up by craftsmen, and the mediaeval thoroughfare in one of the most charming streets in the whole of Brittany. In days gone by, it was also of great economic importance for it led to the port from which was shipped the cloth made by local weavers (there were 1,500 of them at the beginning of the 19th century).

Today, only dredgers and pleasure craft move along the river near the **Old Bridge** (rebuilt in 1923). If you cross the bridge and take the first turning on your right, you will find yourself on the towpath beneath the hill at Lanvallay. This stroll through the **Léhon Meadows** is a delightful way of passing the time. It leads to Léhon Abbey (q.v.).

If you wish to stay longer in Dinan, you might like to walk along the quaysides. On your left, at the northern end just before the road climbs towards Taden, you will see the beautiful terraced estate of **La Grande Vigne** (1830) which is to be open to the public sometime in the future. One of its outbuildings, **La Vignette**, has already been laid out as an artist's studio. Purchased by the painter Yvonne Jean-Haffen in 1937, the property now belongs to Dinan Town Council. The life and works of Mathurin Méheut (1882-1958) and Yvonne Jean-Haffen will remain for ever entwined in a symphony that is, by nature, unfinished, but whose final crescendo was set against the background of La Grande Vigne. The booklet on Yvonne Jean-Haffen written by Denise Delouche is particularly interesting.

At the foot of this estate is the path leading to the valleys of **La Fontaine-des-Eaux**. There were once thermal springs here, and watermills. If you continue to the end of the path, you reach the Dinard road and the Château de la Conninais (cf. Taden).

Another walk would take you along the towpath on the banks of the R. Rance to Le Châtelier Lock (4 m. downstream). You can also take a boat trip along the river from Dinan.

A number of films have been shot in the old town. Among the most recent are *L'Inspecteur Lavardin* (1986) directed by Claude Chabrol, *Promis, Juré!* (1987) directed by Jacques Monnet, and *Les Prouesses de Clément Dujar* (1990) directed by Hervé Baslé.

DINARD (Ille-et-Vilaine)
14m. N of Dinan

The name of Dinard is more mysterious than that of Dinan. Although experts recognise the Celtic root *din* (meaning "a hill"), they lose themselves in hypotheses when it comes to the end of the word. It is highly unlikely that it comes from the Breton *arzh* ("a bear"), even though a bear might have a symbolic importance for the Celts (as shown in the name of King Arthur).

Until the middle of the 19th century, Dinard was still no more than a small fishing village, but it was very busy because it was from here that people crossed the river (the Saint-Brieuc road ended in Dinard). The village was then attached to **Saint-Enogat** further west. But its mild climate and well-sheltered beaches were soon to attract all the idle rich and crowned heads in France and Europe as a whole.

Financiers decided to invest in the resort and very fine villas then began to spring up facing the sea or the Rance Estuary. One of the financiers was a Lebanese man named Joseph Rochaïd, who has given his name to one of the town's squares. English because

Overleaf : *Dinard and the Rance Estuary.*

Bottom : *The Ecluse Beach in Dinard.*

Dinard's second language. The race was on to have the most luxurious villa in which to hold the most extravagant evenings for the in-set. An American by the name of Coppinger even had a castle built here, the "Castel Coppinger". The first casino opened its doors in 1877.

Dinard was at the height of its popularity between 1885 and 1914 (the Cristal Hôtel opened in 1893, and the new casino in 1902). All the great names of the Edwardian Age, from Lady Mond to Picasso, came to Dinard, which was linked by rail to the distant capital in 1887. Debussy wrote his symphonic poem *La Mer* here in 1904. Lawrence of Arabia explored the region by bike and even went to a Jesuit school in Dinard for a short time. Félix

Faure, Edward VII and many others came here to dip their toes in the water or flirt amidst the mimosas, palm trees and tamarisks. And the sand is so soft and the sea so green... In fact, it was Dinard that popularised the name, "Emerald Coast", coined by a local writer, Eugène Herpin, c. 1889.

The town has remained faithful to its vocation as an international tourist centre but it has succeeded in diversifying its attractions (Val-Pirée Riding Stables, golf course, tennis courts, and conference centre). Dinard has a superb Protestant church (1871) and a small **Museum** near Notre-Dame Church. But it is best known for the wonderful footpaths leading from its beaches. To the north, the **Plage de l'Ecluse**, which lies bet-

ween the Pointe de la Malouine and the Pointe du Moulinet, is the largest beach. From there, a footpath along the shore leads to the **Plage de la Prieuré** to the southeast (opposite Saint-Malo). It takes you past the casino, conference centre and aquarium to the Promenade du Clair-de-Lune where, sheltered from the winds, there is an amazing variety of Mediterranean vegetation (palm trees, agaves, and eucalyptus). The best time to walk along this path is on an evening when the moon is full (in the springtime of a love affair) when the loudspeakers of a *son et lumiere* appropriately broadcast Beethoven's *Moonlight Sonata*. From the Prieuré, you can walk to the Pointe de La Vicomté (opposite Saint-Servan).

Showjumping in Dinard.

The Rance tidal power station.

And again leaving from the Plage de l'Ecluse but in the opposite direction, be sure to walk along the water's edge to the beach at Saint-Enogat (you can see the Goule-aux-Fées grotto at low tide) and Port-Blanc. On your way, you will see the "Pré aux Oiseaux", once the home of Judith Gautier, the daughter of the author, Théophile Gautier. Fascinated by the Far East, the highly-attractive Judith decided to settle in Dinard. She died there in 1917 and was laid in her final resting-place in the old cemetery in Saint-Enogat, beneath the sybilline protection of Chinese characters. The novelist Roger Vercel bought "Les Peupliers" in 1936.

The resort has been easier to reach since the building of the dam across the R.Rance (1960-1966) and the **tidal power station.** It began to operate at full capacity in 1967 and it has an annual production of some 600 million Kwh. A swing bridge enables boats to pass through. The site was chosen in 1945 for a well-known reason. In the Rance Estuary, the tide is one of the strongest in Europe (58 ft.). The station was a real technical achievement but it altered the appearance of the banks of the Rance.

The writer Anne de Tourville (b. 1910) now lives in Dinard. Her novel *Jabadao* won the Prix Femina literary award in 1951.

ERQUY (Côtes d'Armor)
15 miles NE of Lamballe

Erquy is one of the main shellfishing ports in France (large catches of scallops in particular are landed here). It is also a bustling seaside resort and has been popular with writers (such as Jean Anouilh and Jean Raspail). Its headland, which consists mainly of pink sandstone, is outstandingly beautiful with its moors and sheer cliff (max. height 221 ft).

Beyond the tiny village of Tues-Roc, amateur archaeologists should look out for the remains of the **Catuélan Ditch** (which protected the tip of the headland

Cap d'Erquy.

in case of attack). It dates from the Iron Age and was later completed by the **Pleine-Garenne Ditch** further to the east. Despite their origins, the ditches are still called "Caesar's Encampment"'. "It's the rich what gets the credit," as the song goes.

At the time of the Coriosolites (cf. Corseul), Erquy was known as Nazado. There was probably a harbour community near the Pointe de la Houssaye. Under the Romans, the town is said to have been called Reginca, or at least so tradition would have it, but experts site this town further east, in Alet to be precise (Saint-Servan) on the banks of the R. Rance (q.v.). In fact, Reginca is said to have been the name of both the river and its main harbour.

The **Château de Bien-Assis** 3 miles to the south (part 15th century but mainly early 17th) still has its crenelated walls, moat, fortified towers and pepper-pot towers.

FORT-LA-LATTE
(Côtes d'Armor)
26 miles NW of Dinan in Fréhel

The fort stands some 195 ft. above the English Channel on a small rocky island separated from the mainland by two gorges. This means that the fortress is virtually impregnable. Despite alteration in the late 17th century carried out by Siméon Garangeau to adapt the fort to the needs of the artillery of the day, it has survived up to the present time without any major changes being made to the original 13th and 14th-century structure. It has been restored by the Joüon des Longrais family which has owned it since 1931.

For many years, Fort-la-Latte was known as La Roche-Goyon Castle, after the family to which it belonged. The Goyon-Matignons, lords of the locality near-by, were to leave their name to the Prime Minister's official resid-

Overleaf : *Fort-la-Latte.*

Château de Bien-Assis.

Cap Fréhel.

ence in Paris. In 1731, one of the Goyon-Matignons married the last heiress of the Grimaldis, thereby becoming Prince of Monaco. Prince Rainier is directly descended from him.

The unassailable appearance of the fortress did not always deter would-be attackers; the Leaguers entered it but were unable to gain control of the keep. In 1715, James Stuart wanted to use it as a base from which to attack the occupant of the throne of England, but the weather was against him. The final siege occurred in 1815 when the Count de Pontbriand's Royalist troops took the fortress, only to be immediately evicted in their turn.

At least two novels are set in Fort-la-Latte, although the setting is revised and corrected by the writer's imagination - *La Châtelaine aux deux visages* (1957) by

Simone Roger-Vercel and *Le Jeu du Roi* (1976) by Jean Raspail.

In 1957, Richard Fleischer filmed *The Vikings* here with Kirk Douglas and Tony Curtis.

Near the fortress is a long thin **menhir** known as "Gargantua's finger".

FREHEL (Côtes d'Armor)
28 miles NW of Dinan

As Bernard Colonne so aptly put it, the first sight of Cap Fréhel is a revelation, *"It is a shock, a strong emotion, a confused feeling of our insignificance when faced with a sight that is both grandiose and tragic, in which water, rock and wind are locked in a pitiless combat"*. Porphyry and red sandstone cliffs tower some 225 ft. above the waters of the Channel, and the

headland is linked to Fort-la-Latte by the **Anse des Sévignés.**

There is a natural sanctuary for migratory birds on the pink sandstone rocks in the small and large **Fauconnière** to the east of the headland. Gulls, seamews, guillemots and cormorants come to nest

40

in the strangely-shaped rocks and cliffs. The best view is to be had from the sea (boats leave Dinard or Saint-Malo). You can also fly over the coast in a helicopter (Dinard-Pleurtuit Airport).

Two **lighthouses** look out over the headland and sea. The older (and smaller) of the two was put into service in the 17th century. The present light was inaugurated in 1950. In fine weather, the light shines over some 62 miles and from the level of the lamp itself the view extends right along the coast and, occasionally, over to the Channel Islands.

Further inland, **Plévenon** ceased to be a community in its own right in 1971 when it was annexed to Pléhérel to form Fréhel. Its modern church (1886) contains a strange stoop with

41

Fréhel lighthouse.

Opposite : *Plévenon.*
The calvary in La Roche-au-Cygron.

Top : *The island of La Fauconnière at Cap Fréhel.*

figures carved in relief. The **calvary at La Roche-au-Cygron** (15th century?) is one of the finest on the Emerald Coast.

Bernard Colonne (b. 1931), poet, seasoned traveller, and French teacher, has settled in Plévenon.

LA GOUESNIERE
(Ille-et-Vilaine)
9 miles SE of Saint-Malo

This village in the Clos-Poulet area midway between the R. Rance and the Baie du Mont Saint-Michel has several manor-

The R. Rance and Lanvallay (right).

houses, but the most interesting building is the **Château de Bonaban**. Built in 1776 for a ship owner named Le Fer de La Sauldre, it is larger than the other shipowners' country residences. It was once a luxurious mansion. Chateaubriand stated that it was famous for its Genoa marble and for "*its magnificence which, even in Paris, we could not imagine*". It was "*decorated with orange groves, fountains of water and statues*".

The artists Dodig and Georges Jégou now live in La Gouesnière.

LANCIEUX (Côtes d'Armor)
12 miles NW of Dinan.

Lancieux is a sort of large peninsula separated from Saint-Jacut by a bay and from Saint-Briac by the Frémur Estuary. This small river should not be confused with another

The town owes its name to a British citizen, Sieu, who came to convert Brittany with his colleague, Brieuc. The **modern church** (1902) is dedicated to him and two stained glass windows depict episodes from his life. Note the **stoup** carved out of a 4th-century Roman milestone; it bears a Latin inscription. In the graveyard stands the belltower (1740) of the original church.

Father Auguste Lemasson (1878-1946), the historian of the Dinan area, was born in Lancieux. The Anglo-Canadian writer, Robert W. Service (1874-1958) died and was buried in Lancieux where he had lived, on and off, for some 40 years. His villa ("Avel Brao") can still be seen on the coast.. Or you can read his detective story *The House of Fear* (1927) which is set in the locality.

On the road to Ploubalay, you can see the Buglais **windmill**.

LANGROLAY-SUR-RANCE (Côtes d'Armor)
8 miles NE of Dinan

The village contains a few remnants of the past that are worthy of note i.e. the Ville-Daniou Cross (of unknown age), the early 18th-century church and, more especially, the **Château de Beauchêne** (18th century). The chateau aroused lyrical descriptions from a local historian, M-E. Monier, *"There emanates from this property a sensation of restfulness and quietude. The tall poplars sing in the wind; in an avenue to the east, the roof of leaves filters the light, which spreads tremblingly across the mossy path, while birds fill the branches..."*

The first owner of the chateau, Jacques Goüin de Beauchêne (1652-1730) was one of Saint-Malo's great navigators. He sailed to the Falklands off Argentina, in 1699.

Langrolay is especially interesting for its beauty spots on the shores of the R. Rance (Pointe du Châtelet, or the shore at Le Morlet).

LANVALLAY (Côtes d'Armor)
1 mile E of Dinan

Lanvallay has been singularly lacking in chance. Standing opposite Dinan, its haughty twin cocking a snook at it from the other side of the Rance, the town seems to have little to offer. Yet it is from the wonderful beauty spot in Lanvallay that you can best admire the Rance Valley and the mediaeval town. The best viewpoints are without doubt the **Mont-en-Val, Lande-Boulou**, or **Château-Monteith**, a British residence whose wide expanse of window in the veranda are an intriguing sight from the Jardin Anglais in Dinan. In the Middle Ages, the hillsides were well-known for their vineyards.

At the bottom of the slope, on the banks of the R. Rance, **La Courbure** was for many years a firm favourite as a place for Sunday picnics. The name, known to have been in existence in 1635, comes from a curve in the river which was easily left to its reed-beds when work was undertaken c. 1828 to lay out a more regular course for the Rance. It is a pity that a factory in Taden now spoils such a wonderful setting.

Even architecturally speaking, Lanvallay has a few buildings of note including the **Château de Grillemont** (16th, 18th and 19th centuries) on the hills of Lande-Boulou, various manorhouses and the tower-dovecot at La Croix-Rolland (17th century). The old **Madeleine District** runs steeply down to the river.

R. Frémur which flows out to the Baie de la Fresnaye. Both names have the same origin viz. the Breton words *froud meur* (large stream). Yet another proof, if such were needed, that Breton was indeed spoken on the shores of the Emerald Coast some 1,000 years ago.

Léhon.

The local population is called "Cotissois", a name that comes from an Upper Brittany dialect word meaning "foxglove", a common plant in the Rance area. For the origin of the name Lanvallay, see Ploubalay.

LEHON (Côtes d'Armor)
1 mile S of Dinan

Six men of God set out to found a monastery. Nomenoë, the then Duke of Brittany, advised them to get hold of holy relics as a first step in their project. The monks eagerly did as they were bid; they sailed to Sark and, during the night, carried off the mortal remains of St. Magloire, Bishop of Dol, who had retired to the island in the latter years of his life (cf. also Pleudihen-sur-Rance). It has to be said, though, that this delightful story is based on a *Life of St. Magloire* written several centuries after the event.

The monastery, of which the earliest features date from the 12th century, underwent a series of ups and downs. Deserted by the monks before the French Revolution, it became a favourite haunt of local youngsters. It was then a cloth mill before being restored in the late 19th century. In 1834, the Brothers of St. John of God had swithered about turning it into a psychiatric hospital. The asylum was indeed built in Léhon but further west, at Les Bas-Foins. It was thought that the nearby river might otherwise have given the inmates ideas! The hospital's foundation stone was laid in 1836.

The abbey church, restored between 1885 and 1897, is 13th century. It has old choir stalls and painted wood panelling dating from the 17th and 19th centuries, several 14th and 15th-century tombstones, and a stoop thought to date from the 13th century. The Beaumanoir Chapel (now the sacristy) houses the remains of what is thought to be the oldest **stained glass window** in Brittany (mid 13th century). Visitors can see the nearby 17th-century cloisters and the 14th-century refectory, which was altered in the 17th century. The 12th-century gateway to the old parish church now stands in the garden next to the minster.

After the publication of the novels of Raoul de Navery (cf. Saint-Hélen and La Vicomté-sur-Rance), popular tradition had it

The old minster in Léhon.

The 17th-century cloisters in Léhon.

Matignon : the Romanesque doorway on St. Germain's Church.

the fortress. It had been badly damaged in earlier fighting. It was rebuilt and it is the ruins of this very late 12th-century and early 13th-century castle that can be seen today. It fell into decline in the late 15th century. It was in the shadow of the castle that the writer Flaubert said he met "*impudent and immodest young girls*".

One-and-a-half miles to the west in the hamlet of Le Saint-Esprit stands a carved **calvary** 26 ft. high, said to date from the mid 14th century.

A road that runs along the banks of the R. Rance upstream from the hump-backed bridge built at the monks' request leads to the **Château du Chesne-Ferron** (16th - 19th centuries), a romantic building overlooking the river.

In **Calorguen** to the south stands the La Ferronays Manor, which was rebuilt in 1569.

MATIGNON (Côtes d'Armor)
15 miles W of Dinard

The town is less well-known than the building in Paris that bears its name (the Prime Minister's official residence). The Matignons, or Goyon-Matignons, are one of the great names in the history of France and Monaco (cf. Fort-La-Latte).

Matignon has at least two manorhouses that are worthy of interest i.e. the Manoir de la Vigne (16th century) and, in particular, the **Manoir de la Chesnaye-Taniot** (17th century). For many years, the town's name was Saint-Germain-de-la-Mer. It lives on in the hamlet of **Saint-Germain** to the north which overlooks the Baie de la Fresnaye. The view over Cap Fréhel is superb and this is an excellent opportunity to take a look at the old tidal-powered mills in the valley. In St. Germain's

that the monks possessed a treasure trove. Nobody has ever found anything but the idea lingers on, as does the belief that a whole network of underground passages runs from the basement of the buildings. It is said that one of the passageways connected the abbey to the ruined fort that overlooked it. The Counts of Dinan took over the site from the Romans, the first people to lay fortifications on **St. Joseph's Hill**, which commanded the river crossing.

The castle was unsuccessfully besieged by Henry Plantagenet in 1168 A.D. but he was an obstinate fellow and returned the following year, when he managed to capture

Chapel (late 19th century), note the remains of a Romanesque porch from the old church.

The doctor to the imperial family in the days of Napoleon III, Antoine Jobert (1799-1867) was born in Matignon ; he became insane at the end of his life. Another local VIP was Paul Sébillot (1843-1918) who collected legends and customs from Upper Brittany - and elsewhere.

LE MINIHIC-SUR-RANCE
(Ille-et-Vilaine)
4 miles SE of Dinard

In Breton, *minic'hi* means "a refuge" or "monastery lands". The name of this village on the banks of the R. Rance, then, proves the existence from very early times of a religious community (doubtless very small in size).

Facing the Saint-Suliac peninsula, Le Minihic has several charming beauty spots e.g. La Landriais, the Promenade des Hures and the Pointe de la Trégondé. A maritime religious procession, or *pardon*, is held here in August, for everybody feels a link with the sea even if times have changed somewhat since Adolphe Orain wrote, in 1882, *"All the young men in the village of Le Minihic are still sailors or ship's carpenters"*.

Le Minihic was the birthplace of Father Louis Lebret (1897-1966), who was a naval officer before becoming a Dominican monk. The brothers Jérôme and Jean Tharaud (1874-1953 and 1877-1952), both members of the Académie Française, used to spend their holidays in Le Minihic, on their estate, "Les Auffenays".

PLANCOËT (Côtes d'Armor)
10 miles NW of Dinan

Plancoët (the "parish in the woods" in Breton) on the banks of the R. Arguenon (q.v.) is full of memories of the youthful Chateaubriand. In his *"Memoirs from beyond the tomb"*, the author described his "first exile" in his grandmother's house. It is still there, on the outskirts of the town, on the Corseul road. Nearby is the strange **House of the Dome** (16th century).

Chateaubriand's maternal relations, the Bédées, also lived in the neighbourhood. Chateaubriand tells how, when he was seven, he was taken to the **Chapel of Our Lady of Nazareth**, to the east, which had been a place of pilgrimage since 1621. Workmen who were busy clearing a well found a broken statue of the Virgin Mary.

Plancoët.

They put it together again but the village idiot threw it back into the well. Thereafter, there were several strange happenings. Moans could be heard coming from the well, a horse was seen to kneel down, and there was a series of unexplained cures.

The chapel dates from 1892. It was built on the site of a 17th-century chapel (one of the towers is still standing) beside a Dominican monastery. Originally, it was called Nozaret; it became Nazareth by a process of assimilation.

Nearby is the spring which provides water sold commercially (Sassay). The millions of bottles marketed annually help to maintain temperance, discreetly but effectively.

To the west of Nazareth are the hills known as La Janière and Brandefer (alt. 296 ft.).

A local man named Pacifique Bossuet, born in 1814, published numerous fables in the style of La Fontaine… but without La Fontaine's genius. Although born in Morlaix, the writer Marie-Paule Salonne (1902-1947) spent most of her life in Plancoët.

PLEBOULLE (Côtes d'Armor)
18 miles W of Dinan

Pléboulle is beautifully situated at the end of the Baie de la Fresnaye. The whole area is filled with beauty spots, for anybody who takes the time to discover them, especially around the **Port-à-la-Duc** and the headland at Crissouët (cf. also Matignon).

St. Paul's Church dates partly from the 18th century and has some interesting furnishings (including a stoop which is a historic monument in its own right).

The Dome House in Plancoët.

Pléboulle church : the stoop.

Pléboulle church : the stoop.

But the chapel of **Notre-Dame du Temple** to the south, in the village of the same name, is more attractive. It was part of a commandery belonging to the Knights Templar. The 14th-century chapel contains wonderful modern stained glass windows and various statues (including a painted statue of the Virgin Mary). Legend has it that one of the three statues of the Madonna and Child shed tears when English soldiers appeared during the Battle of Saint-Cast (q.v.).

To the west flows the shy Frémur (for the meaning of the river's name, cf. Lancieux). Standing proudly on the edge of the Roman road linking Carhaix and Corseul, **Montbran Castle** is in fact a polygonal keep, now in ruins, dating from the early 13th century. This is one of the oldest architectural remains in the area. An annual fair, the Temple Fair, whose origins date back to the Middle Ages, is held in September beneath the walls of the castle. It used to last for ten days!

The Chapel of Notre-Dame du Hirel in **Ruca** to the south dates mainly from the early 16th century. **Saint-Pôtan**, further to the east, contains the castles of La Ville-Even (17th century) and Le Vauméloisel (early 18th century).

PLESLIN-TRIGAVOU
(Côtes d'Armor)
5 miles N of Dinan

The name Pleslin many come from the Breton *"lenn"* in which case it would mean "the lakeside parish", and there is indeed a small lake in the village. The church, which is of no especial interest, has some old furnishings and an old font (13th century).

Nearby (if you come from Dinan, turn left to La Ville-Crochu) are five rows of standing stones, a total of 65 **menhirs**, jutting out from the undergrowth on the Champ du Rocher.

To the west is the town of Trigavou. There is some question of its name having a connection with goats (*"gavr"* in Breton). Whatever the truth of the matter, the **corbels** in the church tell the story of a chase involving a wolf and a goat. Moreover, tradition has it that it was the goat which caught the wolf. The church, built from 1310 onwards, was altered in the 17th century. It contains a head-shaped reliquary of St. Bridget (late 17th century).

Outside, along the south wall, are the tombstones of the squires of the Bois de la Motte. Standing to the west of Trigavou, the house is an asymmetrical manor built mainly in the 17th century. The surrounding ditches serve as a reminder that the builders originally intended it to be a fortress.

PLEUDIHEN-SUR-RANCE
(Côtes d'Armor) *7 miles NE of Dinan*

For centuries past, Pleudihen has been famous for its cider. Indeed, it has a **Cider and Apple Museum**. Tradition has it that the monks from Léhon (q.v.) stopped on the banks of the R. Rance for a rest on their way back from Sark. They put St. Magloire's relics in an apple tree in Pleudihen and, although it was winter, the tree immediately began to produce fruit.

To the west, nor far from the Rance, is the **Ville-Ger** strand which was once well-known for its cockles, and the **Mordreuc Plain** opposite the towers of Le Chêne-Vert (cf. Plouër).

The author Jean Mordreuc (1908-1982) was born in Pleudihen. He is known for his short stories and novels. The historian André Mussat (1912-1989), who was an unrivalled expert on Breton architecture, settled in Pleudihen.

PLEURTUIT (Ille-et-Vilaine)
4 miles S of Dinan

This is a large village or small town (pop. 4,500) of very ancient origins (as shown by its Breton name whose meaning remains unclear). Nowadays, Pleurtuit is best-known for its **airport**, which is totally unfair. The town has a number of sights including manor-houses and, in particular, a luxurious *malouinière*, a country house built for a Saint-Malo ship-

Pleurtuit Airport.

owner, the **Château de Montmarin** (18th century) which is remarkable for its Italianate roof, its sumptuous interior decoration, and its formal gardens. It is one of the few *malouinières* on the left bank.

On the shores of the R. Rance, Pleurtuit was once famous for the construction of bisquine fishing smacks (cf. Cancale). But times are not what they once were and you will have to make do with the **Pointe de Cancaval** or the slipway at **Jouvente**. M-E. Monier wrote of the town in 1953, "*Everything has the beauty of youth here, with a slight touch of nonchalance and romantic verse*". You can even stop at the pub if you are so inclined.

Dr. François Broussais (1772-1838), although born in Saint-Malo, spent his childhood in Pleurtuit (cf. also Dinan).

The great pilot, Marcel Brindejonc des Moulinais (1982-1916), was born in Saint-Brieuc but spent part of his short life in Pleurtuit. He is buried there, near the present airport.

PLOUBALAY (Côtes d'Armor)
2 miles S of Lancieux

Ploubalay is a large, prosperous farming community which is also famous for its horse-racing - and its water tower restaurant (338 ft. in height) from which there is a superb view. There are a number of castles and country houses within the boundary of Ploubalay including **La Coudraye** (1729).

Balay is not one of the better-known Breton saints, but his name is found again in the village of Lanvallay near Dinan.

Plessix-Balisson, which is totally surrounded by Ploubalay, is the second-smallest community in mainland France after Castel-moron-d'Albret (Gironde). It has an area of 8 hectares 26 ares and 80 centiares and a population of 94, which makes it the least-populated community in the Dinan and Emerald Coast area. The church (1919) has a 15th-century doorway.

PLOUER-SUR-RANCE
(Côtes d'Armor)
6 miles NE of Dinan

The men of the Plouër region (the "parish of St. Hern" in Breton?) once enjoyed the reput-

The banks of the R. Rance below La Souhaitier.

ation of being excellent sailors. Not that this prevented them from keeping their feet firmly on the ground, and being skilled craftsmen. The carpenters were just as capable of building a ship as they were of putting up a roof. Some of them even knew how to use more precious wood to make violins.

The church (late 18th century) has two 14th-century tombstones. The castle dates from the 17th century. There used to be a Protestant church in Plouër, built in the late 16th century but it was demolished in 1664 by the Catholic clergy. The village had had an active Huguenot community. But the main attraction of the village is its nearness to the

Top : *La Souhaitier.*

Opposite : *Château de Monchoix, Pluduno.*

minded and expert ladies to amuse the guests after the excellent meal. Kowalski would then seat himself at the piano and improvise voluptuous music to suit the comings and goings of the gentlemen and their partners from the bawdy house. A taste of days long gone.

St. Hubert's Bridge (1959) and the **Chateaubriand Bridge** (1991) span narrows partway along the Rance and link Plouër and Taden to La Ville-es-Nonais (q.v.). They also provide a magnificent view over the river as it widens out to the south, forming the Mordreuc "plain", the maritime plain stretching lazily from Plouër to La Ville-es-Nonais and Pleudihen.

Further north, the **La Souhaitier Maritime Chapel** opposite Saint-Suliac is yet another place of pilgrimage. A *pardon* is held here in August. It is a very old place of pilgrimage. The present chapel dates from 1868 but was preceded by one built in 1670. This proves the extent to which the communities in the Rance Valley as far as Dinan had a maritime basis in days gone by.

The sculptor Louise Leroux-Druet, who was born in Dinan in 1898, is also a writer. One of her novels, *A deux pas de la cale* (1958) which she wrote under the pen-name Elisa Mauny, describes Plouër and the banks of the R. Rance. The artist Pierre Rochereau (b. 1910) was born in Dinan but now lives in Plouër.

To the north-west of the centre of Plouër is the **Lémon Rock** (or Lesmont Rock) which has matrimonial virtues. Girls who slide down it wearing their baptismal breeches may well find themselves a husband before the year is out. Well, you can always try, preferably on a night when the moon is full.

Rance Estuary. Overlooking the river opposite the Mordreuc "plain", the **towers of Le Chêne-Vert** seem to come straight out of a novel by Ann Radcliffe.

The towers had just been restored when the pianist, Henri Kowlaski (1841-1916), settled in the nearby Château de Vaucarhel. According to Gabriel-Louis Pringué, this Parisian musician whose father was Polish but whose mother came from Dinan, was Chopin's last pupil. His biographer further mentions that he had a finely-developed sense of oecumenism. He taught music in Dinan and played for Mass as well as for other, less austere occasions. *At that time, the sub-prefect who governed Dinan proved to be quite a lad. He would invite Kowalski to important men-only lunches and, once the meal was over, would go out to the steps down to the garden with a hunting horn on which he would blow a loud fanfare. The local brothel would hear the call and immediately send over open-*

PLUDUNO (Côtes d'Armor)
13 miles NW of Dinan

Everybody knows, or should know, Chateaubriand's description of the **Château de Monchoix** in the first few pages of his *Memoirs from beyond the tomb*. This was the home of his maternal grandparents, the Bédée de la Bouëtardais.

"The Count of Bedée's castle," he wrote, *"lay a league from Plancoët, on a delightful hillside. Everything was impregnated with a feeling of joy. My uncle's sense of humour was endless (...) Monchoix was filled with cousins from the neighbourhood. There was music, dancing, hunting, everybody enjoyed themselves from morning to night (...). Going from Combourg to Monchoix was like travelling from the desert into the world, from the keep of a mediaeval baron to the villa of a Roman prince"*.

The Château de Monchoix (1759) is still Pluduno's pride and joy. There is also a 16th-century manorhouse within the community, **Le Bois-Feuillet**.

LE POUDOUVRE
(Côtes d'Armor)

This is a vast region stretching from the Channel in the north to the Arguenon and Rieule in the west and the Rance to the east. Only its southern boundary seems uncertain. Its name is linked to its rivers (*pagus daoudour*, or land of waters) and it corresponds to the *pagus aquensis* of Gallo-Roman times. This being so, the term "Poudouvre" covers the Dinan area (in fact Dinan is the main town) but excludes the entire right bank of the R. Rance. Although little used today, the name seems to be reserved rather

more for the inland area than the coastline.

The Poudouvre has certainly been French-speaking or Gallo-speaking (the language of Upper Brittany, but with numerous local dialects) for a thousand years or more. But various place names indicate that this was not always so. Names like Arguenon, Frémur (cf. Lancieux), Pleurtuit, Plouër, Taden, Calorguen, Aucalaeuc, Quévert, Créhen, Languenan and Trigavou are obviously

Top : *The R. Rance in Chantoiseau in Saint-Hélen.*

Overleaf : *The R. Rance near Le Châtelier.*

of Breton or Celtic origin, even if their meaning is not always clear. The name "Dinan" is thought to be of Celtic origin (it also exists in Belgium), meaning "hill" or "defensive site" (cf. Dinard).

THE RIVER RANCE

Côtes d'Armor? Ille-et-Vilaine? Administrative divisions are made for government and are artificial, whereas on the banks of the Rance, there is nothing to distinguish between the two *départements*. A feature that could have been a natural frontier, the river, does more to unite the Poudouvre and Clos-Poulet areas than to separate them. The left and right banks are non-iden-

59

The R. Rance near La Vicomté.

tical twins, responding to each other, complementing each other, in a dazzling array of colours with a predominance of green. It is no exaggeration to describe this as an entity, a different "civilisation" which has developed over the centuries in an emerald green fjord, a natural scar of earth and rock.

The valley is unique for its double current, with the river flowing towards the estuary and the tidal current flowing inland (the tide is one of the strongest in the world). The birth of the river is, of course, linked to the long geological history of Armorica (a period of glaciation followed by a rise in the level of the sea as it pushed southwards). The banks consist mainly of gneiss, except for a long tongue of shale cutting diagonally across the area from Langrolay to Cancale.

The meaning of the name is unknown but it may have its origin in Reginca (cf. Erquy), which could have become "Renc" in the 9th century.

Rising in Collinée, in the Méné Moors deep in the heart of eastern Brittany, the 50-mile R. Rance starts life as a mere stream. It does not become a river for some distance, although the manmade Rophémel Dam near Guitté gives it short-lived vigour. It is in Evran, where it joins the Ille-et-Rance Canal, that the Rance begins to widen out, backed up by the waters of the Guinefort and Linon rivers. Beyond the curve at Tressaint (Pont-Perrin), it flows on to the lock at Léhon then, "*in the green fissure of a steep-sided plateau*", slips between Dinan and Lanvallay. From here to the estuary, it passes through 17 towns and villages. On the left bank are Dinan, Taden, Saint-Samson, Plouër, Langrolay, Le Minihic, Pleurtuit, La Richardais and Dinard. The right bank has Lanvallay, Saint-Hélen, La Vicomté, Pleudihen, La Ville-es-Nonais, Saint-Suliac, Saint-Jouan, and Saint-Malo (q.v.)

Beyond Léhon, the Rance becomes a maritime waterway. Or

Top : *La Ville-es-Pois and Le Châtelier (opposite).*

Overleaf : *La Hisse.*

at least, it was until the tidal power station was built. The tide used to flow as far as the Dinan area and it was not uncommon to catch shrimps at the bottom of the Jerzual. For centuries, the sea and river organised everyday life in this area. Now, it is difficult to imagine the hustle and bustle that existed for so long on the quay-sides and towpaths. It was the Rance that imported and exported all types of goods. It was the Rance that brought Dinan into contact with the coast, the Channel Islands and more distant horizons.

For many hundreds of years, the Rance was the route used by barbarians, conquering troops, missionaries, merchants, "soldie-ry and capitains". And it was this "royal waterway", as Gérard Malherbe so prettily describes it, that took the Crusaders on the first stages of their journey from Dinan to the Holy Land. Much later, local lads from Pleudihen, Plouër and Saint-Hélen, set off along the Rance to become ships boys and sailors.

The water level was not the same as it is today and fords or scantily-built bridges enabled pedestrians to cross the Rance (almost) without getting their feet wet, for example where the Asile des Pêcheurs stands today in Taden (originally an important river port). Navigation on the Rance was much more difficult than it is today, now that work has been undertaken to correct the somewhat anarchic course of the waterway (this is obvious in the long agonising meanders, now forgotten and slowly disap-pearing beneath the mud and reed beds).

Beyond Dinan, the most beau-tiful town in Brittany, the Rance gradually becomes a narrow ria, overlooked here and there by hill-sides, some of them very steep. Here, said François Ménez, "*rich vegetation spreads across the landscape, less Breton than Norman in style, full of placid fertility, with orchards and pastures*". But the Rance can also

take its time, spreading into a lake when the shores are less hostile. These lakes are described as "plains" (Taden, Mordreuc). Then, after one last line of hills (and if you shut your eyes as you cross the dismal dam), comes the majestic arrival at the Emerald Coast on which the eye immediately catches sight of two architectural gems with quite different charms - Dinard and Saint-Malo. *"Like a departing ship, shortly before it casts off from the mainland"*.

It is not sufficient to cruise up the Rance, or fly over it in a helicopter, if you want to know it properly. You have to walk along its shores or the towpath (as far as possible). Each view is different. Each shoreline has its own charms, each creek its own mystery. And each season, of course, brings its own light to bear on a natural environment that is constantly changing. Here and there, humble dwellings or prestigious country houses bear witness to the presence of man - menhirs, churches, chapels, castles, towers, hermitages, and *malouinières*. It would take a lifetime to see all the beauties of the enchanted valley. But it takes much less time to appreciate its delights. Yet there is nothing very spectacular about it. Beauty makes no attempt to scale heights here; it retains its human dimension.

The slipway at Mordreuc and Le Chêne-Vert.

LA RICHARDAIS
(Ille-et-Vilaine)
2 miles SE of Dinard

This is the first town visitors come across as they head southwards from the Rance Dam. The shores were once a hive of activity here, where shipbuilding used to be the main trade.

The church was decorated with frescoes (1953) by Xavier de Langlais. The Manoir de La Motte belongs to Charles Dédéyan (b. 1910), a literary critic. Those who are interested in neither literature nor art may prefer to visit the **Pointe de la Goujeonnais**.

Les Sables-d'Or.

Overleaf : *Saint-Briac.*

SABLES-D'OR-LES-PINS
(Côtes d'Armor)
26 miles NW of Dinan

It would take a clever man indeed to decide whether Sables-d'Or-les-Pins is part of the Emerald Coast - or the Penthièvre Coast (a more recent name). The town is certainly closer to Lamballe than Saint-Malo but it was a man from Saint-Malo, Roland Brouard (1887-1934), who created this seaside resort out of nothing c. 1922. This area of shoreline, though, had been lived in for many years and proof has been found of Gallo-Roman settlements.

Brouard suffered financial ruin in the operation despite its success. Bernard Colonne described the first days of Sables-d'Or, "*In 1925, the resort opened. There were hotels, casinos, golf courses, tennis courts, riding clubs, all of them attracting a wealthy clientele that soon gained an international dimension. There was an open-air theatre which attracted actors as famous as Pierre Fresnay and Yvonne Printemps...*"

Plurien to the south-east, has a Romanesque **church** which underwent major restoration in the 14th century and again, to an even greater extent in the 19th. The singer, painter and poetess Maripol was born in Plurien in 1945. She now lives in Fréhel.

69

Saint-Benoît-des-Ondes.

SAINT-BENOIT-DES-ONDES
(Ille-et-Vilaine)
5 miles S of Cancale

This is the boundary, marked by the stream known as the Biez Jean, between the Clos-Poulet and the Dol area. Saint-Benoît, which lies on the Baie du Mont Saint-Michel, is part of the great "marshland" known to locals of old as "maraous". In those days, the landscape was dotted with **windmills**. In Saint-Benoît, they have all disappeared.

It was a Benedictine monastery founded in the Middle Ages which gave its name to the community. The church dates from the late 18th century and St. Genevieve's Chapel from the 16th.

The name Biez Jean contains the old French word *biez*, which has given the modern French word "bief" i.e. mill-race.

SAINT-BRIAC-SUR-MER
16 miles NW of Dinan

This town, which gets its name from St. Briac (cf. Saint-Lunaire) is a pretty seaside resort in a ria at the mouth of the R. Frémur. There is a fine view of the harbour from the Armel-Beaufils Gardens.

Not that delightful views are in short supply. The **Emerald Coast Belvedere** is an elegant

Saint-Cast.

cliff road. The village has several beautiful beaches e.g. Le Béchay, La Salinette, and Port-Hue. Despite its Romanesque appearance, the **church** is modern but its tower dates from the 16th century. A bridge across the R. Frémur leads to Lancieux.

Georges Nivat, a specialist in Russian literature and translator of Soljenitsyne, spends his summers in Saint-Briac, in the Pont-Martin Mill. And (is this a coincidence?) Grand Duke Vladimir of Russia, heir to the throne of the tsars, also lives in Saint-Briac, where the imperial family has been resident since 1921.

Henri Le Saux (1910-1973), who was born in Saint-Briac, became a monk in Brittany before setting off for India. He has written a number of books on Hindu spiritualism.

SAINT-CAST-LE-GUILDO
(Côtes d'Armor)
12 miles NW of Dinan

Launched during the Edwardian era, like Dinard, the resort of Saint-Cast developed at a slightly later stage - and much less spectacularly. Its rival enjoyed the proximity of Saint-Malo and Dinan, not to mention a railway station.

Saint-Cast, though, was by no means inferior to Dinard and

The castle in Le Guildo.

The main beach.

several great artists e.g. Bernard Buffet or Julien Gracq, realised this very well. The town has several beaches, the main one extending over a mile between the **Pointe de la Garde** and the headland in Saint-Cast itself. There is an observation platform near the headland.

The town has two distinct areas. To the north is the seaside resort of Saint-Cast; to the south is Notre-Dame-du-Guildo (from the Breton *"goueled"* meaning "lower section"), a peaceful, slightly more rural hamlet on the banks of the R. Arguenon.

Pointe de la Garde.

In the 18th century, Saint-Cast was the scene of a major battle. On 11th September 1758, the French won a victory over the English and Welsh (who showed little inclination to fight the Bretons anyway). Some people have questioned the exact role played by the Duke d'Aiguillon, Governor of Brittany, who was supposed to be in charge of the forces fighting the invader. According to La Chalotais, Advocate General to the Parliament of Brittany, *"the French army gained all the glory and the Duke d'Aiguillon got nothing but egg (and flour) on his face"*. He meant that the military chief-of-staff was actually busy flirting with a miller's wife while battle raged, having set up his headquarters in the mill. Let he who hath never sinned, throw the first stone...

It was at the **Pointe de la Garde** that Julien Gracq rediscovered *the stark purity of line that resembles a garden in the evening after it has been watered, a Japanese etching in which the damp foliage and rocks are not hidden by wisps of mist, or Roscoff on certain mornings after a night of rainfall.*

On the left bank of the Arguenon are the **ringing stones**. They are, in fact, amphiboles which jingle when they are tapped with a different mineral. On the right bank, i.e. within the boundary of Créhen, are the remains of Le Guildo Castle, now undergoing restoration. It was in the early 15th-century fortress that the young Prince Gilles of Brittany lived. He was brought up in the English Court, decided to settle in Le Guildo, and there led a joyous existence with his British friends. His ambitions brought him into conflict with his

75

brother, Duke François I. Believing Gilles to be in the pay of the English, the Duke had him arrested and declared that he *wished Mr. Gilles might be in Paradise.* The prince was strangled in 1450. His rollicking lifestyle is traditionally said by the locals to be the origin of the expression "*courir le guilledou*" ("to play the field") but it is a doubtfully chauvinistic explanation.

The writer Hippolyte de La Morvonnais (1802-1853) lived for many years in the **Château du Val d'Arguenon** (late 18th - early 19th century). Some of its rooms have been turned into B & B accommodation. The estate runs down to the shore. The 17th-century **manor** was a monastery of the White Friars before the French Revolution. The monks became boat-owners and made a profit out of the river crossing the days when there was no bridge spanning the waterway. From Le Guildo, you can also go to **Quatre-Vaux beach**, which used to be popular with Romans living in Corseul.

As you head back to Saint-Cast from Quatre-Vaux, it is worth stopping at **St. Bridget's Chapel** (13th-century windows), at Penguen Beach or at the **Pointe du Bay**, the last prong of what Loïc-René Vilbert nicknamed "the Saint-Cast trident" (the headlands at Saint-Cast, la Garde and Bay).

The author Michel Tal Houarn, a short story writer and novelist, was born in Saint-Cast in 1926.

Saint-Cast : Pointe de la Garde.

SAINT-COULOMB
(Ille-et-Vilaine)
3 miles W of Cancale

The **Château de La Fosse-Hingant**, which is also still known as the Château de Néermont, stands at the west end of Saint-Coulomb on the Paramé road, near the Sainte-Suzanne lake. This was the cradle of the Breton conspiracy against the Convention. The castle owner, Marc Désilles de Cambernon, was the treasurer of the organisation run by La Rouërie. His son, André, had been killed in Nancy in 1790, when he threw himself in front of the cannons to separate the National Guard and the troops who had remained loyal to the king. In 1793, the conspirators were betrayed by a doctor friend, a man above suspicion, Valentin Chévetel. He had revealed all the details of the plot to Danton and a detachment of the National Guard came to conduct a search of La Fosse-Hingant. Using the information supplied by Chévetel, the soldiers discovered papers relating to the conspiracy hidden in a jar.

One of Désilles' daughters, Angélique de La Fonchais, then aged 24, was mentioned on the list. She died on the scaffold in Paris, with eleven of the conspirators. As to Marc Désilles, the owner of La Fosse-Hingant, he succeeded in escaping to Jersey where he died in despair. Jeanne, his wife, became insane. Valentin

Overleaf : *Ile Duguesclin in Saint-Coulomb.*

Opposite : *A panoramic view from the Pointe du Meinga.*

79

Chévetel became the Mayor of Orly and did not die until 1834. He had married an actress, the former mistress of La Rouërie. The heart has its reasons...

On the other side of the lake is a Regency-style *malouinière*, **La Mettrie-aux-Houets**. The town is, in fact, full of manorhouses and country seats. Among the finest are **La Ville-Bague** to the north-west (on the La Guimorais road) and the **Château du Lupin** (1692) overlooking the moorings at Rothéneuf.

La Guimorais has a number of beaches and beauty spots. The authoress, Colette, who was a frequent visitor to the Saint-Malo area between 1911 and 1924, used to live in the **Manoir de Rozven** above the Touesse Cove. She used this setting in her novel, *Le Blé en herbe* (1923).

The **Ilot du Chevret** is a bird sanctuary. To the north-east, in the **Du Guesclin cove**, is a tiny island with the remains of a fortress. The singer, Léo Ferré, lived in the fortress during the 1960's. To the south is **Le Plessis-Bertrand**, which was built in 1259 and demolished in 1589.

SAINT-GUINOUX
(Ille-et-Vilaine)
10 miles SE of Saint-Malo

This village on the edge of the Saint-Coulban lake has kept alive memories of Pierre de Maupertuis (1698-1759), a member of the French Academy, who had a manorhouse here. He was a brilliant mathematician, and was born in Saint-Malo. He introduced into France the Newtonian theory of gravity and paid for an expedition to the polar ice cap to measure the Meridian. Frederick II of Prussia invited him to Berlin where he chaired the Academy.

He met up with Voltaire there and the two brilliant minds quickly crossed swords!

The artist and art publisher Pierre Derveaux (born 1945 in Saint-Malo) has settled in Saint-Guinoux.

SAINT-HELEN
(Côtes d'Armor)
6 miles NE of Dinan

There are few people who know that Saint-Hélen, which stretches out over a long distance

The ruins of Coëtquen castle, in Saint-Hélen.

a romantic windmill), there is a panoramic view of the surrounding countryside. In particularly fine weather, the view extends as far as Mont Saint-Michel.

The Neogothic **church**, which was gutted by fire in 1941, has little of interest other than tombstones bearing coats-of-arms. However, there are the remains of Paleolithic industry in the village of La Ganerie (to the north-west) and, of greater interest, the ruins of a castle to the east on the edge of the Coëtquen Forest which has a large number of birch trees (hence perhaps its name, said to mean "white wood"). The fortress has suffered many misfortunes. Built in the mid 15th century on older remains and altered in the 17th century, it was demolished by Revolutionary troops in 1794 for fear that it might be used as a hideout by the Royalist Insurrectionists.

Coëtquen has had a reputation of being accursed ever since the publication of a book by Raoul de Navery, the virile pen name of Adèle, known as Eugénie, Saffray (1828-1885) whose trilogy, *Patira, Le Trésor de l'abbaye* and *Jean Canada* (1875-1887) enjoyed enormous success in the region. In *Patira* (repub. 1990) the author tells how a young woman was said to have been locked up in the castle dungeons. The story was based on a romantic tale published in Dinan in 1836, recounting a series of strange discoveries made in the late 18th century. In those days, everybody could recite by heart the opening words of *Patira*, "*Coëtquen Castle, one of the most magnificent in the Dinan area, resounded on that morning to the joyous sounds of the hunt setting out....*"

The poet and publisher Yves Prié (b. 1949) and the artist Jean-

(1,640 hectares) has a discreet access to the Rance, to the west of the Croix-du-Frêne. It is a creek filled with reedbeds, known as **Chantoiseau**, overlooking Taden. Thanks, perhaps, to this window on the outside world, there was a time not so very long ago when many of Saint-Hélen's young men joined the Navy.

It is true that the village is situated further east, very much inland. From the **mound** (where a hideous water tower has replaced

Luc Chauvin (b. 1954) both came from Saint-Hélen. It is not unusual to see Denise Delouche there, an expert in the history of art (in particular, painting in Brittany). Her house stands next to the forest.

Also on the edge of the forest, but in Ille-et-Vilaine, is the beautiful **La Chênaye** Estate on which the writer Félicité de Lamennais once lived.

SAINT-JACUT-DE-LA-MER
(Côtes d'Armor)
14 miles N of Dinan

Seen from a plane, the meagre Saint-Jacut peninsula looks like no more than a mirage. Yet this "discreet Finistère" as Jacques Petit so prettily described it, is one of the most popular places on the Emerald Coast - and one of the least spoiled. On condition, of course, that you take the time to stroll along the shores and beaches from south to north of the peninsula (overlooking the Baie de Lancieux) and from north to south (overlooking the Baie de l'Arguenon). When the gods and lighting are favourable, take a walk from the Pointe du Chevet to the Banche and from the Banche to Vauver before going on to the ruins of Le Guildo. It is an unforgettable experience. Nature has, miraculously, been untouched here.

Saint-Jacut.

Top : *The Ile des Ebihens in Saint-Jacut.*
Overleaf : *An aerial view of Les Ebihens.*

The noise and fury of everyday life seems to have been abolished for all time, and sages in search of true emotion will at last be able to enjoy a momentary taste of eternity.

The main street is the backbone of the village. It is lined by stocky houses in "rows" turning their backs on the northerly winds. Cut off from the world, huddling on their peninsula and nursing their abject poverty, the locals of old used to inter-marry, speak their own dialect and, in most cases, go fishing for mackerel. If Paul Sébillot is to be believed, their fishwives used colourful language and were quick to raise their hands in anger.

Ancient Breton tradition had a firm belief in heredity. Thus Jacut (or Jagu) belonged to a family which did not trifle with sainthood. He was the son of St. Fracan and St. Gwenn, and the brother of St. Guthenoc and St. Winwaloe. Jacut studied on the island of Lavret then came to this peninsula with Guthenoc to found the first monastery. That, says tradition, was in the early years of the 6th century.

Thereafter, the abbey of Saint-Jacut (which, with Landévennec, was one of the oldest in Brittany) was to become a Benedictine monastery of high repute. The cult of St. Jacut spread throughout Armorica and people prayed to him for assistance in cases of rabies, insanity and possession by the Devil. Dom Alexis Lobineau (1667-1727), one of Brittany's first historians, came to work in this monastery and stayed there until his death. The great consecrated menhir in the cemetery is reminiscent of Dom Lobineau's grave. A few decades later, the abbey disappeared for ever, a victim of the French Revolution. Today, the Abbaye guest house stands on the site.

Offshore, **Ebihens Island** (20 hectares) has a fortified tower. Coriosolite coinage (cf. Corseul) has been found on the island, with the remains of a village dating from the 1st century B.C. The **island of La Colombière** to the west is a bird sanctuary.

The poet and painter Guy Mahé was born in Saint-Jacut in 1929, as was the artist Louis Guillard (born 1924). The poet

Jacques-G. Krafft (1890-1960) spent the last few years of his life in Saint-Jacut.

As you head back inland, you can see, on the outskirts of **Trégon** on the Créhen road, a 52 ft. long passage grave, in the hamlet of La Hautière.

SAINT-JOUAN-DES-GUERETS (Ille-et-Vilaine)
4 miles SE of Saint-Malo

Well-situated on the shores of the R. Rance between Saint-Servan and Saint-Suliac, the small town of Saint-Jouan has a number of manors or *malouinières* dating from the 17th and 18th centuries, e.g. La Ville-es-Oris.

You might like to take a stroll along the riverbank, beside the **Tertre**, near the Val-es-Bouillis, or on the headland at La Roche-du-Port. The tiny islands of Chevret, Notre-Dame and Harteau lie within the town's boundary.

SAINT-LORMEL
(Côtes d'Armor)
11 miles NW of Dinan

The banks of the Arguenon. "*The banks,* wrote François Ménez, *"gradually widen out between Saint-Lormel and Créhen, trimmed with hills topped here and there by a clump of pine trees twisted by the wind from the sea*".

A stop in Saint-Lormel provides an opportunity to see St. Lunaire's Chapel (former church) built in a composite style, with a 12th-century Romanesque doorway. There is a very fine stoop inside the chapel.

Anybody interested in history and architecture can see the **Manoir de la Ville-Robert** (17th century) which, during the One Hundred Days, was the headquarters of a royalist leader, Colonel Le Pontbriand (1776-1844). The **Château de Largentaye** (1840) has connections with the Rioust des Villes-Audrains family, one of whose members succeeded in halting an army of 10,000 English soldiers in Le Guildo, in 1758.

A small chapel in Le Val-es-Bouillis.

The R. Rance seen from Saint-Jouan-des-Guérets.

SAINT-LUNAIRE
16 miles NW of Dinan

The **church** (partly Romanesque but with major restoration) contains the tomb of St. Lunaire, an Irish bishop who brought Christianity to the area in the 6th century. The Gallo-Roman sarcophagus was covered, in the 14th century, by a granite slab depicting the bishop in his vestments. Note the dove on his chest. It is an allusion to the legend of the saint. While crossing the Channel, the boat was caught in a terrible storm but the priest continued to sleep. In order to lighten the load, his companions threw a number of objects overboard, including the sacred stone on which the Bishop celebrated Mass. When Lunaire landed in Armorica, two doves flew down and laid the stone at his feet. The recumbent figure is supported by the remains of Romanesque carvings.

The cliffs along the Emerald Coast used to be the haunt of the fairy folk (cf. La Goule-es-Fées in Saint-Enogat), elves, mermaids with golden tresses, and the ghost ship of Captain Black, a phantom condemned to sail the seas and indicate the arrival of storms by lighting his ship's lanterns.

From Saint-Lunaire, you can go northwards to the **Pointe du**

Saint-Lunaire.

Décollé. This is the centre of the Baie de Saint-Malo, in the very heart of a half-hoop of beauty. There is a superb view of Saint-Malo harbour (to the east) and the headlands at Saint-Cast or Cap Fréhel (to the west). The **Pointe de la Garde-Guérin** further west also provides visitors with a striking view.

The musician Ivan Devriès, a descendent of Théophile Gautier, was born in Saint-Lunaire in 1909. The actor, Jean Rochefort, has been coming to the resort regularly since his childhood.

SAINT-MALO (Ille-et-Vilaine)
37 miles N of Rennes

"A stone diadem floating on the waves", said Flaubert, and Saint-Malo really does lie in an exceptional setting at the mouth of the R. Rance. Originally, it was just an island linked to terra firma by a sandbank that was covered by the sea every day. The rock was connected to Paramé in the 18th century by the causeway known as Le Sillon. The former tidal basin was replaced in 1930 by a wet dock and a dyke with a lock. Sébastien Vauban wanted to begin work on the project as far back as the 17th century but he ran up against local opposition. For many centuries, Saint-Malo was a centre of the Newfoundland fishing fleet; now its commercial harbour trades mainly with the British Isles and it is also a major ferry terminal.

Towards the middle of the 6th century, a Welsh monk named Machutus alias Maclaw (or Malo) landed on the rock with a view to bringing Christianity to the people of Aleth (now Saint-Servan). He

Saint-Lunaire.

Top : *The small keep in Saint-Malo.*

Overleaf : *Saint-Malo.*

became their Bishop. After ministering to them for several years, the Bishop of Alet decided to retire to this rock then, having aroused ill-feeling among some of his parishioners, Malo left the area for the Saintonge Region where he died c. 627 A.D. His relics were returned to the island a century later.

In order to flee from the invasions by the Franks and, later, the Vikings, the people of Aleth would seek refuge (as their Bishop had done before them) on the rock to which they had given his name. It was not until the 12th century that Jean de Châtillon

Duguay-Trouin (Saint-Malo Museum).

transferred the diocesan seat here. The town of Saint-Malo-en-l'Isle was born.

Saint-Malo owes its exceptional wealth to its people whose passion for overcoming any obstacle in their way and whose spirit of independence led to their motto, *Malouin first and foremost, Breton perhaps, French only if there's anything left.* The Malouin character really does

exist, created by centuries of battles on land and sea. The people still show a will to master their own destiny. During the War of Succession, they refused to recognise Jean de Montfort as Duke of Brittany. Defended by the privateer, Morfouace, and by Bertrand Du Guesclin, the town withstood attack by the Duke of Lancaster, who was forced to lift his siege. Although Jean IV finally succeed-

ed in quelling the whole of Brittany, he never controlled the rebel town. The people of Saint-Malo supported their bishop, Josselin de Rohan, who intended to be answerable to none but the Pope. After all, Rome was so far away... It was not until Jean IV blockaded the town and had the Solidor Tower built in Saint-Servan that the locals finally capitulated. But as soon as they had an opportun-

Preparations for the transatlantic Rum Route yacht race.

ity to do so, they placed themselves under the jurisdiction of the King of France.

In 1415, Charles VI returned Saint-Malo to the new Duke of Brittany, Jean V, who was a loyal subject. Mistrusting the ebullient town, he had the keep built, rather more as a means of monitoring the locals than as a means of defending them. In order to establish her authority and ensure obed-

ience, Duchess Anne strengthened the castle and had engraved on the tower, *"Whoever complains shall obey, for such is my will"*. With the marriage of Anne and King Charles VIII, followed by her marriage to King Louis XII, the people of Saint-Malo gained French nationality. But they remained first and foremost *"malouins"*.

In the 16th century, during the

days of the Leaguers, they captured the castle and set up an independent aristocratic republic. It lasted for four years, during which time the town provided its own seaward defences and sent ambassadors to Spain and Portugal. In the 17th century, Saint-Malo was France's foremost harbour. It owed its prosperity to wide-ranging maritime trade based on cod-fishing off Newfoundland, which

Bon-Secours Beach.

Saint-Malo : La Houssaye.

had been discovered by one of its inhabitants (Jacques Cartier), and the fur trade with Canada. Salt cod was sold in the countries bordering the Mediterranean. The ships then loaded their holds with alun from Rome which they delivered to the textile centres of Northern Europe. They also dealt in canvas and cotton with India and Spain. In the South Altantic, the Falkland Islands were visited by a local navigator named Gouin de Beauchesne in 1699; he named them "Îles Malouines". In the 18th century, the locals were involved in the Slave Trade and they controlled the islands of Bourbon and France (now Réunion and Mauritius).

The difficult political and economic situation in which France found itself at the end of Louis XIV's reign forced the Malouins to turn to a substitute form of trade that has been glorified in legends, i.e. privateering. Joint stock companies commissioned pirate ships in order to overcome the deficiencies of general trading. It was at this time that Sébastien Vauban and Siméon Garangeau completed the building of the town's defences and the forts on the rocks that surrounded the bay (Fort Royal, Petit-Bé, Ile Herbois, Conchée, Cézembre, Ile Harbour etc.), all of them reefs that made the town impregnable. The English swore to destroy this arrogant town of merchants and pirates, in order to weaken Louis XIV. They never succeeded in doing so!

During the French Revolution, Saint-Malo became known as Port-Malo. The harbour's commercial activities continued to decline. Surcouf was perhaps the most famous of the privateers but his exploits were isolated events. The golden age of the privateer was over. But Saint-Malo had not

yet done with tragedy. Of all the attacks and fires that the pirate city had to withstand during its long, troubled history, the most devastating was the huge blaze that wiped out 80% of the town in August 1944. Today, though, Saint-Malo has been skilfully rebuilt in the monumental style of the town houses first erected in the 18th century by Garangeau.

Enter the walled town by St. Vincent's Gate. The **castle**, now the town hall, dates from the 15th century except for the eastern section, the Gallery, which was built in the 17th century. The **Quiquengrogne Tower** backing onto the small keep was commissioned by Duchess Anne. The **Great Keep**, which was completed during the days of Duke Jean V and which was extended by the addition of the massive tower known as the "General" is now the **local museum**. Exhibits retrace the history of the privateers' town and its famous men.

A walk round the ramparts is quite magnificent, and it is the best way to see Saint-Malo. The walls (which were not destroyed by the great fire of August 1944) were the work of Siméon Garangeau, Vauban's pupil. It should, however, be pointed out that the north-western section between the Bidouane Tower (17th century) and the Queen's Fort (18th century) was built last century. Beyond the Bidouane Tower stands the statue of Robert Surcouf, pointing towards England. The western section of the walls, which face seawards above Bon-Secours Beach, date from the Middle Ages; these are the smaller walls commissioned by Bishop Jean de Châtillon, which stretched from the Bidouane Tower to the Holland Bastion. Beyond it is a statue of Jacques Cartier.

A general view from the castle.

The main street and the cathedral.

The St. Vincent Gate.

Le Grand-Bé with Chateaubriand's grave.

Opposite, top : *Factory ships.*
Opposite, bottom : *The Cavalier Bastion.*

From the walls, the string of rocks surrounding the town is quite visible - the **Petit-Bé** with its fort and the **Grand-Bé** where the writer François-René de Chateaubriand is buried. The word Bé is said to come from the Breton "bez" meaning "a grave" and it is quite likely that the Celts considered these islands as maritime cemeteries where the souls of the departed met after death. Further out to sea are Cézembre where the monks once lived, La Conchée Fort (1695), and **Fort-Harbour**, both of them designed by Sébastien Vauban.

A few of the houses escaped fire damage in 1944 e.g. the Magon de la Lande and Asfeld Residences near St. Louis' Gate.

The granite shipowners' houses were designed by Garangeau in the 18th century. The **La Gicquelais Residence** (Chateaubriand's birthplace) and the "glasshouse" (a wood and glass construction dating from the 16th century) in the Rue Pélicot were also able to be saved. The buildings near the Dinan Gate to the west were rebuilt.

St. Vincent's Cathedral has now been fully restored by Raymond Cornon and Pierre Prunet. It shows a combination of styles from various periods (12th to 20th centuries). The West Front includes Renaissance, Classical and 18th-century architecture. The 12th-century nave is roofed with great ogival arches in the

style of the Anjou region, while the 13th-century chancel is typical of the Anglo-Norman style that is common in Brittany. The wonderful **great rose window** (1969-1972) was designed by Jean Le Moal and Bernard Allain, while the windows in the side aisles are by Max Ingrand.

This small town (its area, according to Chateaubriand, was not even equivalent to that of the Tuileries Garden in Paris) was the birthplace of a large number of famous men with stubborn temperaments, including Jacques Cartier (c.1494-1557), René Duguay-Trouin (1673-1736), Bertrand Mahé de la Bourdonnais (1699-1753), François-René de Chateaubriand (1768-1848), Robert Sur-

105

In St. Vincent's Cathedral.
On previous pages : *The town walls and shipowners' houses.*

couf (1773-1827), and the two Lamennais brothers, Jean-Marie (1780-1860) and Félicité (1782-1854).

Like many of the towns in the Rance area, (cf. Dinan and Dinard), Saint-Malo has always been attractive to the British. An Englishwoman, Anna Snell, came from India and lived here for some time in the second half of the 19th century before moving to Le Mans and becoming a novelist in the French language. Her works are now forgotten - but the name of her grandson is well-known. He too was a writer, Somerset Maugham. In his novel *The Magician* (1908), Maugham described a pure-bred Breton who was proud of his ancestry, Dr. Porhoët (cf. Chapter 13).

Saint-Malo has become an ultramodern seaside resort with excellent sports facilities (golf courses, tennis courts, swimming pools, flying club, sailing schools etc.). It also has a **marine hydrotherapy centre**.

The Sillon Causeway.
Overleaf : *Saint-Servan and the Solidor Tower.*

SAINT-SERVAN

Saint-Servan used to be called Alet and the surrounding area was the Clos-Poulet (q.v.). The large Gallo-Roman town became the capital of the Coriosolites (cf. Corseul and Erquy) and **Gallo-Roman sites** are numerous in the neighbourhood. One of them, at the foot of the Solidor Tower, dates from 390 A.D. The area was once covered by woodland that gradually disappeared beneath the waves. Tradition has it that it was a tidal wave which swamped the forest in 709 A.D.

After being pillaged and set ablaze on several occasions during the Viking invasions, Alet was outranked in the 12th century by Saint-Malo. The **Solidor Tower** was built in 1382 by Duke Jean IV of Brittany to keep control of the pirate town and prevent it from trading with Dinan. Solidor, which consists of three adjoining machicolated towers, is a fine example of mediaeval military architecture.

The Solidor Tower.

Le Bosc.

Today, it houses the **Cape Horners Museum**. It is worth taking a stroll along the cliff path that runs round the peninsula; there are some outstanding views of Saint-Malo, Dinard, and the Rance Estuary.

La Briantais Manor on the banks of the river is a cultural meeting-place and seminar centre. It used to belong to a politician named Guy La Chambre (1898-1975) who was a cabinet minister in several governments.

Saint-Servant has several fine *malouinières*, such as **Le Val-Marin** which is typical of the 18th-century style and **La Verde-**

La Chipaudière.

rie, whose turret is reminiscent of Renaissance buildings. It was built in the 17th century for Noël Danycan, who founded the "South Sea Trading Company".

Near Saint-Jouan-des-Guérets but still in Saint-Servan, in Quelmer on the banks of the R.Rance is **Le Bosq** (1717), one of the most beautiful of all these country houses. It was built for a family of shipowners, the Magon de la Lande.It stands in the middle of a park facing the R. Rance and is open to the public during the peak holiday season. This would be an appropriate place to read, or re-read, Roger Vercel's *La Hourie* (1942).

PARAME

Now linked to Saint-Malo by the Sillon Causeway, Paramé is a large seaside resort. Take a stroll along the esplanade that follows the main beach and enjoy the picturesque scenery. When the tide is exceptionally high, the waves crash in across the road. Round about Paramé, there are a number of country houses. **Les Chênes** on the outskirts of the town has connections with Chateaubriand. Legend has it that he carried off his young fiancée from here, in the purest romantic tradition. The truth, though, is quite different. Young René, who was rather hos-

tile to the idea of married life, let himself be wed by his sisters! *"In order to avoid one hour's argument,"* he wrote, *"I have allowed myself to be enslaved for one century"*. He took what consolation he could and merely noted one day, *"My wife is so confident in my talent as a writer that she has never felt the need to read one line of what I have written in order to convince herself further"*.

In the depths of the country stands **La Chipaudière**, the most beautiful country house in the Clos-Poulet. François Magon de la Lande, a shipowner from Saint-Malo, had it designed by

Garangeau c. 1715 (it is not open to the public).

The village of **Rothéneuf** has a **sea life centre** and a few remains of Jacques Cartier's country house, the Portes-Cartier Farm. The writer Théophile Briant (1891-1956) is buried in Rothéneuf, having spent the last twenty-two years of his life in the Saint-Malo area.

It was on a **rocky headland** that dips down to the sea that Father Fouré (1839-1910) sculpted the legend of the Rothéneuf family. It took him 25 years to complete. The granite poem stretches over an area of 598 sq. yards and depicts some 300 characters. The Rothéneufs were pirates and fishermen-smugglers, who lived here in the mid 16th century. For one hundred years, they enjoyed the respect of their influential neighbours in Saint-Malo. The priest has turned this tribe into a strange portrait gallery, a Gargantuan fresco that is the pinnacle of naive poetry.

Not far from the headland is **Rothéneuf Haven**, one of the most delightful spots on the coast. At high tide, it is a small lake much appreciated by water sports' enthusiasts; at low tide the sea goes right out, leaving a fine beach.

Paramé was the birthplace of the composer, Louis Aubert (1877-1968) who left a number of symphonic poems and instrumental works. The illustrator Robert Velter (alias Robvel) who created the character, Spirou, in 1938, retired to Paramé.

Rothéneuf.

115

The carved rocks at Rothéneuf.

The 16th-century **Limoëlou Manor** is now a Jacques Cartier Museum.

SAINT-MELOIR-DES-ONDES
(Ille-et-Vilaine)
4 miles SW of Cancale

This large community, which was already a hive of activity in Gallo-Roman times, overlooks the Baie du Mont Saint-Michel. In the Middle Ages, it was the seat of a priory that depended on the wealthy abbey. Today, within the boundaries of the community, there are various manorhouses and castles of varying interest. In particular, there are two *malounières*, **Le Bouillon** (1730), and **Val-Ernoult** (1719) which be-

came the property of the Robert-Lamennais family (that included Félicité and Jean-Marie).

The Saint-Méloir area is very fertile and specialises in market gardening. The town has even become one of the largest early vegetable centres in France.

Its daily market is of major importance, specialising in potatoes and cauliflowers in season. The economic dynamism explains the increase in its population from 2,322 in 1982 to 2,588 in 1990. The town has a **glass-blowing workshop** in the Rue Radegonde.

SAINT-SAMSON-SUR-RANCE (Côtes d'Armor)
4 miles N of Dinan

Like many other local towns and villages, Saint-Samson stands on the banks of the R. Rance, on the top of a hill. It used to be known as Saint-Samson-Jouxte-Livet, a reference to Livet which is one of the spots along the river (cf. La Vicomté-sur-Rance).

The **La Tiemblaye menhir**, which is decorated with Neolithic symbols and engravings, is one of the finest standing stones in the Dinan area. It is thought to have stood here for the past 5,000 years.

One of the most unusual spots along the shores of the R. Rance lies between La Hisse and the Lessary Bridge. If the light is favourable, the river ceases to be Breton, with its square fishing nets and their platforms, and takes on a Far Eastern charm.

The Dol-Dinan railway crosses the river on the **Lessart Bridge** (1879, rebuilt in 1950 after the air raids of 1944). In 1887, it took 9 1/2 hours to travel by train from Paris to Dinan.

Saint-Samson was the home of François Hingant de la

Saint-Suliac.

Thiemblaye (1761-1827), Chateaubriand's companion in exile in Great Britain, where he tried to commit suicide with a penknife. Chateaubriand describes the episode in his *Memoirs from beyond the tomb*. Hingant wrote a number of unpublished works. The manuscripts are kept in the town library in Dinan.

SAINT-SULIAC
5 miles SW of Saint-Malo.

Saint-Suliac was a settlement in prehistoric times and several implements from the Mousterian have been discovered here. Today, it is a picturesque harbour on the banks of the R.Rance, where narrow streets of granite houses run steeply down to the jetty.

The **church** on the top of a rise is a remarkable building that shows English influence. In fact, the general setting has something British about it with its old graveyard (it still has a few old tombstones), its cypress trees, its lawn, and the view over the river from the close. The church dates partly from the 13th century, which is fairly unusual in Brittany. On the north side is a square tower with a massive buttress. Also on the north side is a porch with ribbed ogival arching which seems to be a precursor of the Apostles' Porches of Lower Brittany. This one contains six statues including four dating from the 13th century (albeit restored since then). To the right of the West Front (17th century) is a strange granite head, perhaps representing St. Suliac.

The Welsh monk, a follower of St. Samson, built a monastery here in the 6th century. Legend has it that he rid the area of a dragon which was terrorising the local population (cf. Chêateauneuf-d'Ille-et-Vilaine). The parish still has the saint's relics and the precious lid of his stone coffin.

Inside the church, note the engaged pillars, various objects or carvings relating to the fishing industry and the modern stained glass windows.

A sight not to be missed on the eastern and southern sides of the old graveyard are the two **gateways** with pointed pediments. They date from the 13th century and are, therefore, the oldest of their kind in Brittany. Saint-Suliac is of especial interest because it has a close, even though it lies within Upper Brittany (and it even used to have an ossuary).

Gargantua stayed in this area for a while. The rocks of **Mont Garot** (alt. 234 ft) provided him with dentures and the other stones in the neighbourhood were pieces of gravel that he shook out of his shoes. In the village of Chablé, there is a menhir 16 ft. high called **Gargantua's Tooth**. While daydreaming, Gargantua even killed his offspring here. Seeing what he had done, the locals killed the murderer in his turn and he was buried on the spot. However, it took so much

earth to fill in his grave that its removal created the Baie de la Baguais. Mont Garot is said to be his burial mound. In the cove at Vigneux, there used to be a menhir called Gargantua's Bed.

Local tradition has it that Vigneux was also a town which disappeared beneath the waters of the R. Rance.

The Gargantua character plays a major role in topographical folk-

Taden : the church and La Grand-Cour Manor.

Although somewhat fanciful, this popular etymology contains a grain of truth which has been retained in local memory inasmuch as Taden lay on a major communication route, probably a Roman road. Nowadays, it has been proven (by Loïc-René Vilbert and Loïc Langouët) that a Roman road ran from Corseul to the Asile des Pêcheurs on the Rance, forded the river and continued eastwards through the Port-Josselin valley. Taden was, in fact, from the 1st century A.D., a *vicus*, i.e. a major river port, and this has been confirmed by aerial photographs (they reveal numerous Gallo-Roman buildings, including two temples). Nearby, the **Taden slipway**, which is well laid out, has been a favourite haunt of local people from Dinan for years (cf. La Vicomté).

The village has two fine 14th-century buildings, which is very rare in this region - the **church** and **Grand-Cour Manor** with its strange watchtower. Another interesting building, the **Manoir de la Conninais** stands much further to the south-west, on the outskirts of Dinan, on the Dinard road. It lies within an estate owned by a bank. Old iron gates, carved lintels, Renaissance windows, a dovecot, an ornamental well, a chapel and a park all give the manor elegance and delicacy. Building began in the late 15th century but alterations were made on several occasions. The defensive tower at the entrance, the "Tower of Love", dates from the 15th century.

The **Château de Kerrozen** (19th century) on the CD 12 is a Neogothic building which was used as a set in the film *L'Inspecteur Lavardin* (1986).

You should not leave the vast but elusive territory of Taden (2,100 hectares) without trying to

lore (cf. Fort-La-Latte). He is, of course, the traditional Gargantua, who existed long before Rabelais' character. Paul Sébillot (cf. Matignon) devoted a study to this figure in 1883.

TADEN (Côtes d'Armor)
3 miles NE of Dinan

There are those who say that the name Taden means "the father of paths, or old path" in Breton.

119

find, on the Ploubalay road (just over one mile from Dinan station) the **ruins of La Garaye**. After a brilliant carefree life, Claude Marot, a native of Rennes, decided to devote himself to the suffering of others, for he had lost a loved one. He became a surgeon and, in 1710, turned his manor-house into a hospital. He gave shelter to the sick and wounded for more than forty years, and died in 1755 at the age of eighty.

The empty building fell into decay at the end of the 18th century but what has survived is full of charm. In the frontage are carved windows and a doorway with columns on each side. The polygonal newel staircase with its decorated openings is a slender construction (early 16th century). Overall, there is a general impression of melancholy. *"Soon,"* said Luigi Odorici in 1857, *"all that will remain of this Renaissance building will be its memory"*. How wrong you were, Mr. Odorici!

In **Trélat** (3 miles N of Dinan), a hamlet within the boundary of Taden, there is a 17th-century chapel containing a 15th-century Madonna and Child. The statue was intended for the abbey in Saint-Jacut but it refused to go any further. Indeed, it became so heavy that it had to be taken off the cart then and there.

The Fishermen's Rest in Taden.

121

Top : *Chateaubriand Bridge.*

Opposite : *Château de la Garaye, Taden.*

LA VICOMTE-SUR-RANCE
(Côtes d'Armor)
5 miles NE of Dinan

This town is often linked to Pleudihen, its near neighbour, of which it was a part until 1878. Its only architecturally-interesting building is the **Manoir de la Bellière** which stands near a lake. The manor was built in the late 14th century but older sections are thought to date from the 13th century. Once a fortress, it is now a pleasant country house. Its defensive system has disappeared.

This is said to have been the birthplace of Tiphaine de Raguenel, Du Guesclin's first wife. It was certainly in the manor chapel that she married him, in 1363. "*Tiphaine was beautiful and knowledgeable; Bertrand was ugly and ignorant. They were bound to make a happy marr-iage*" said Roger Vercel in his biography of the Constable. He obviously believed in the doubtful virtues of marriages of opposites.

Although poor in reminders of the past, La Vicomté is far from lacking in attractions, because the R. Rance runs close by. Take a trip to the lock at **Le Châtelier** (or Le Livet) linking the twin areas of La Vicomté and Saint-Samson (q.v.). For decades, this little corner of the Rance was one of the main meeting places for people from Dinan. Every Sunday after Mass, they would travel here in serried ranks, on foot or by bike. A wonderful scent of pancakes and sausages rewarded them for their efforts.

To the south is the **Le Châtelier hillfort**, which is especially visible from a plane. The promontory above the river is a delightful, popular spot. Opposite it are the sheer rocks of Taden which were used as the setting for Chapter 20 of *Patira*, the novel by Raoul de Navery (cf. Léhon and Saint-Hélen) under the name of "the Dinâmmas gibbet". One of the characters in the book, Tanguy de Coëtquen, climbs the rocks before throwing himself off the top - just as a group of priests

were sailing by in a boat, singing the *Deo profundis* !

LA VILLE-ES-NONAIS
(Ille-et-Vilaine)
6 miles SW of Saint-Malo

This tiny community on the banks of the R. Rance got its name from a Benedictine priory. The monks settled in a spot that became known as Port-**Saint-Jean**, opposite Port-Saint-Hubert in Plouër. The Rance is very narrow here, scarcely more than 420 ft. The **Chateaubriand Bridge** (1991) now links the two banks and enables drivers to go on to Plouër or Dinan. The original bridge (1959) was not sufficient for the task. There used to be a ferry run by the Knights Hospitaller of St. John, which brought them in a few dividends. The setting is superb.

The **Manoir de Vauboeuf** (early 17th century) was built on the shore.

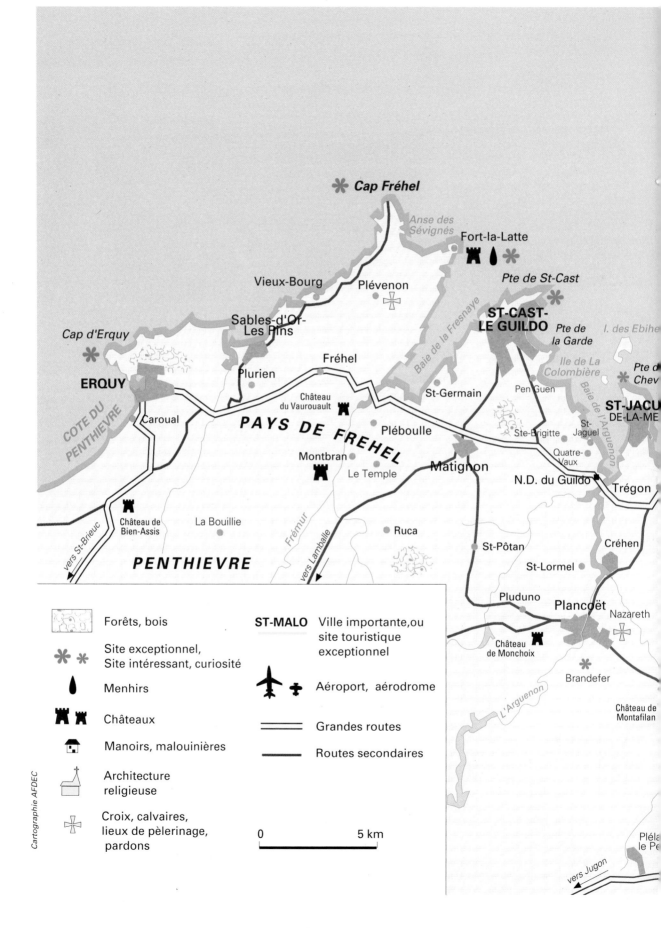

* Cap Fréhel

Anse des
Sévignés

Fort-la-Latte

Vieux-Bourg

Plévenon

Pte de St-Cast

Sables-d'Or-
Les Pins

Baie de la Fresnaye

ST-CAST-
LE GUILDO

Pte de
la Garde

Cap d'Erquy

Fréhel

I. des Ebihe

Ile de La
Colombière

Pte d
Chev

ERQUY

Plurien

St-Germain

Pen Guen

ST-JACU
DE-LA-ME

Baie de l'Arguenon

COTE DU
PENTHIEVRE

Car0ual

PAYS DE FRÉHEL

Château
du Vaurouault

Pléboulle

Ste-Brigitte

St-
Jaguel

Montbran

Le Temple

Matignon

Quatre-
Vaux

N.D. du Guildo

Trégon

Château de
Bien-Assis

La Bouillie

Frémur

Ruca

St-Pôtan

Créhen

vers St-Brieuc

vers Lamballe

St-Lormel

PENTHIEVRE

Pluduno

Plancoët

Nazareth

Forêts, bois

ST-MALO Ville importante, ou
site touristique
exceptionnel

Château
de Monchoix

* * Site exceptionnel,
Site intéressant, curiosité

Aéroport, aérodrome

Brandefer

L'Arguenon

Menhirs

Châteaux

Grandes routes

Château de
Montafilan

Manoirs, malouinières

Routes secondaires

Architecture
religieuse

Croix, calvaires,
lieux de pèlerinage,
pardons

0   5 km

Pléla
le Pe

vers Jugon

Cartographie AFDEC

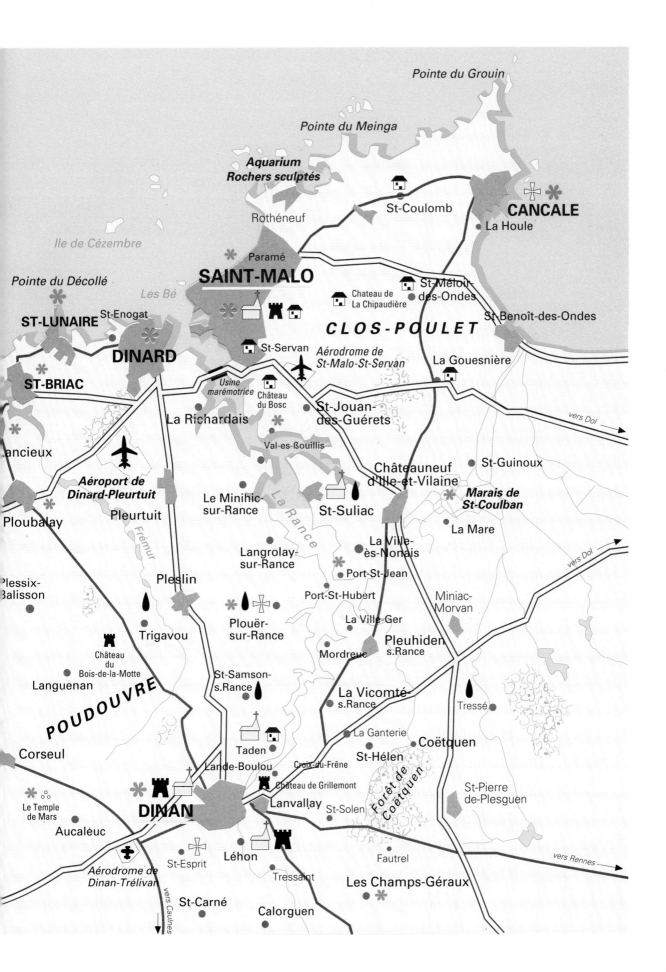

TABLE OF CONTENTS

A BRIEF BIBLIOGRAPHY

AMIOT (P.). - *Histoire du pays de Fréhel*, available from the author, 1981.
BANEAT (P.). - *L'Ille-et-Vilaine historique, archéologique, monumentale*, Larcher, Rennes, 1927.
BERNADES (A.). - *Origine et évolution de Cancale et sa région*, Chambrin, Cancale, 1989.
BROSSE (J.), chief editor. - *Dictionnaire des églises de France*, Vol. 4, Laffont, 1968.
BUFFET (H-F.). - *En Haute-Bretagne*, Librairie Celtique, 1954.
CATHERINE (C.). - *Ille-et-Vilaine*, Siloë, Laval, 1987.
CHARDRONNET (J.). - *Histoire de la Bretagne*, Nouvelles Editions Latines, 1965.
COLONNE (B.). - *Le Pays de Fréhel*, Ouest-France, 1986.
DAGNET (A.). - *Le Clos-Poulet* (1907), Rue des Scribes, 1988.
DAGNET (A.)A - *La Rance* (1911), Rue des Scribes, 1988.
DELOUCHE (D.). - *Yvonne Jean-Haffen*, Bibliothèque municipale, Dinan, 1990.
DERVEAUX (D.). - *Gentilhommières du pays de Saint-Malo*, Editions Derveaux, Saint-Malo, 1961.
GAIGNARD (H-G.). - *Visages de Rance*, Lanore, 1983.
LANGOUET (L.). - *Les Coriosolites : un peuple armoricain*, Centre régional d'Archéologie d'Alet, Saint-Malo, 1988
LEGARDINIER (C.). - *Promenade littéraires à Saint-Malo* , Ouest-France, 1990.
LESPAGNOL (A.). - *Messieurs de Saint-Malo : une élite négociante au temps de Louis XIV*, L'Ancre de Marine, Saint-Malo, 1991.
MALHERBE (G.) and VILBERT (L-R.). - *Dinan en cartes postales anciennes*, Bibliothèque européenne, Zaltbommel (Netherlands), 1974.
MALLET (M.). - *Dinard sur la Côte d'Emeraude*, Jos Le Doaré, Châteaulin, 1988.
MENEZ (F.). - *Rivières bretonnes*, Calligrammes, Quimper, 1990.
MONIER (M-E.). - *Quinze promenades autour de Dinan*, Imprimerie bretonne, Rennes, 1956.
MUSSAT (A.). - *Arts et culture de Bretagne : un millénaire*, Berger-Levrault, 1979.
ORAIN (A.). - *Géographie pittoresque du département d'Ille-et-Vilaine*, Alphonse Le Roy Fils, Rennes, 1882; Laffitte Reprints, Marseilles, 1982
ROBET-MAYNIAL (D.). - *Tourisme en Ille-et-Vilaine*, Nouvelles Editions Latines, undated.
RUAUX (J-Y.). - *Dinan et son pays*, Editions des Templiers, Dinan, 1989.
RUAUX (J-Y.). - *La Côte d'Emeraude*, Ouest-France, 1977.
SAINT-JOUAN (R. de). - *Dictionnaire des communes : département des Côtes-d'Armor*, Conseil Général des Côtes d'Armor, Saint-Brieuc, 1990.
VALLAUX (C.), WAQUET (H.), DUPOUT (A.), et CHASSE (C.). - *Visages de la Bretagne*, Horizons de France, 1941.
VERCEL (R.). - *La Rance*, (gouaches by Jean Urvoy), Editions Arc en Ciel, 1945.
WAQUET (H.). *L'art breton*, 2 vols., Arthaud, Grenoble.

I should also like to mention the excellent annual publication entitled *Le Pays de Dinan* (town library, Dinan) directed by Loïc-René Vilbert. Readers will find an additional bibliography in the **New Guide to Brittany** (Ouest-France, 1984).

May I thank Loïc-René Vilbert for his suggestions and those who, in 1976, were my first assistants in the Emerald Coast and its hinterland, Jean-Yves Ruaux and Bruno Sourdin.

My grateful thanks, too, to those who first introduced me to the Dinan area and its delightful valley, my parents **Pierre and Madeleine Renouard**. It is also appropriate to mention my crystal-clear memories of my uncle, **Raymond Leforestier** (1911-1957) alias the Hermit of Coëtquen, teacher of literature, musician, storyteller and chronicler. He was my first guide.

M.R.

Cet ouvrage a été imprimé par l'imprimerie Mame à Tours (37)
I.S.B.N. 2.7373.0795.3 - Dépôt légal : juin 1991
N° éditeur : 2107.01.05.06.91